Real World

Colouring Book

For Advanced Users & Adults

50 Images

Created From Real Life Photos
For You To Colour As You Please.

ISBN 978-0-359-83336-8

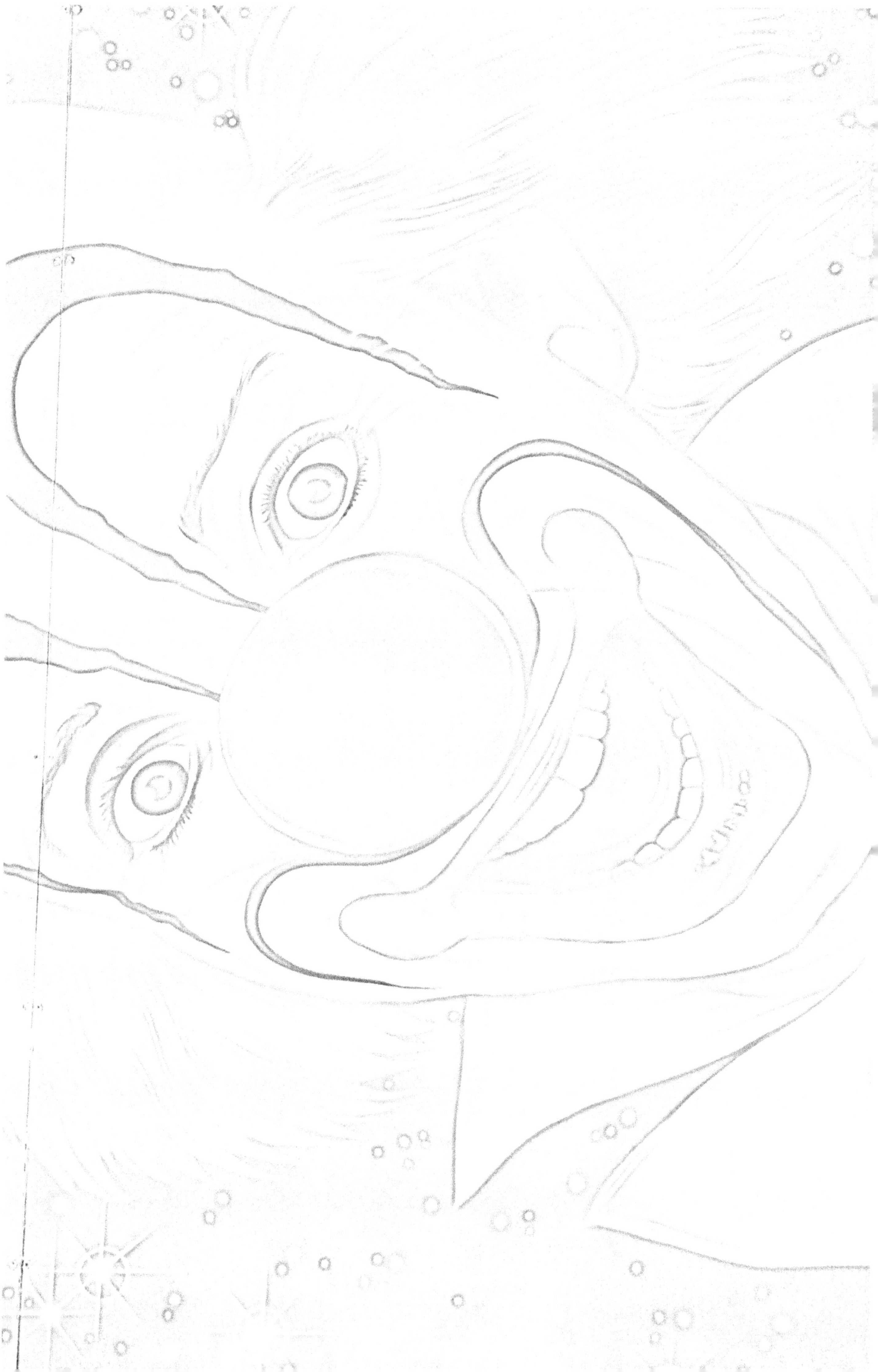

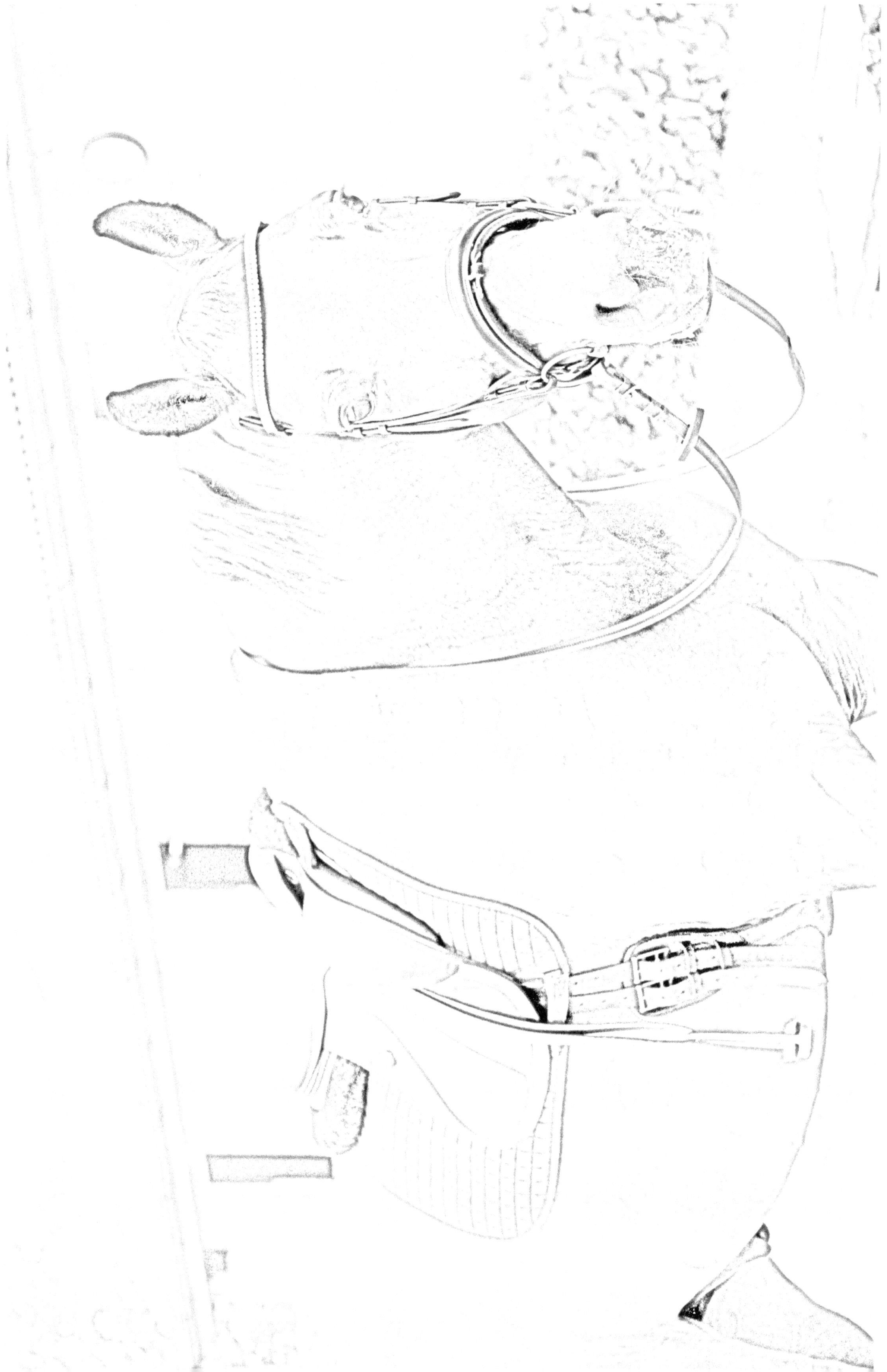

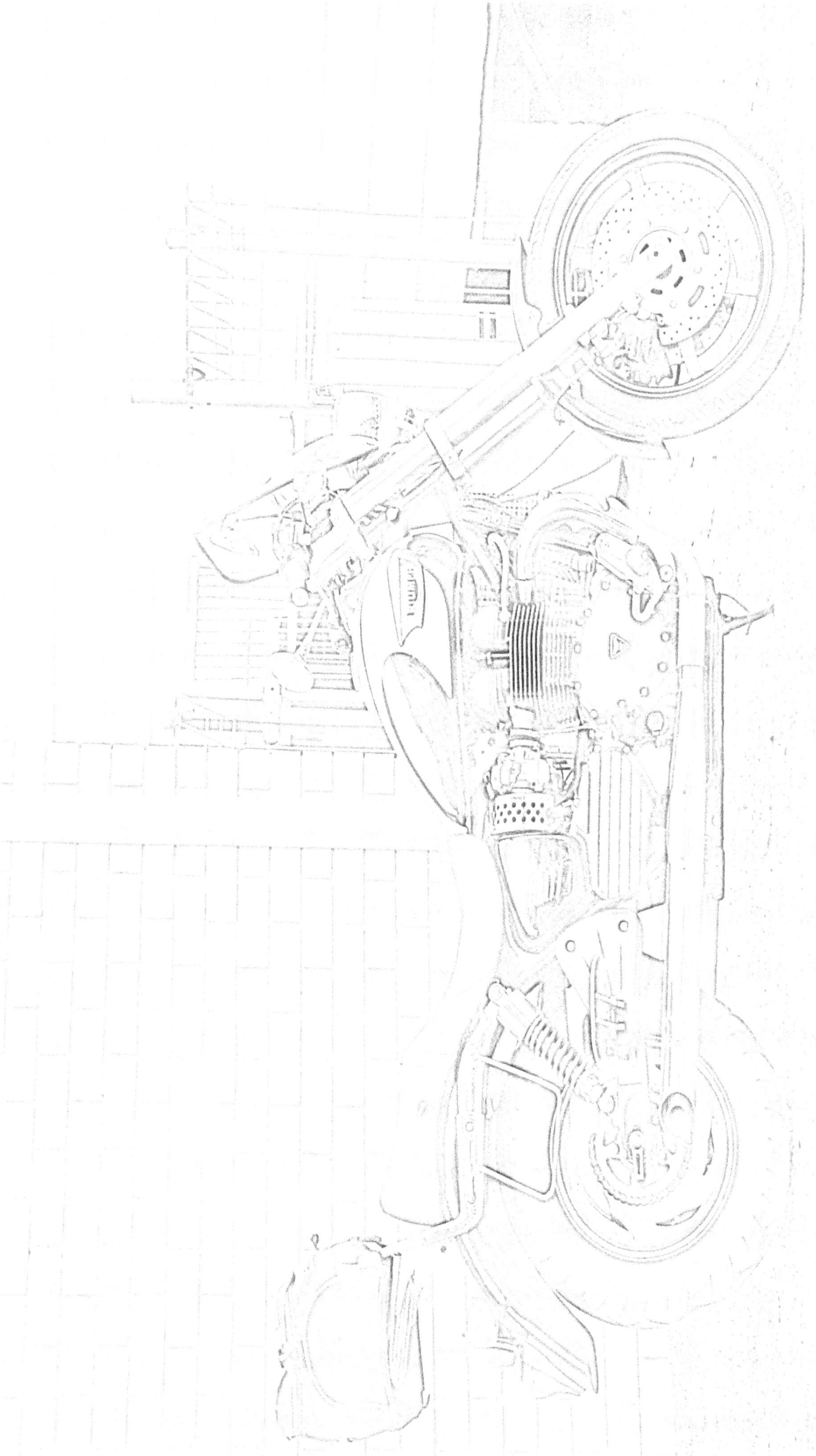

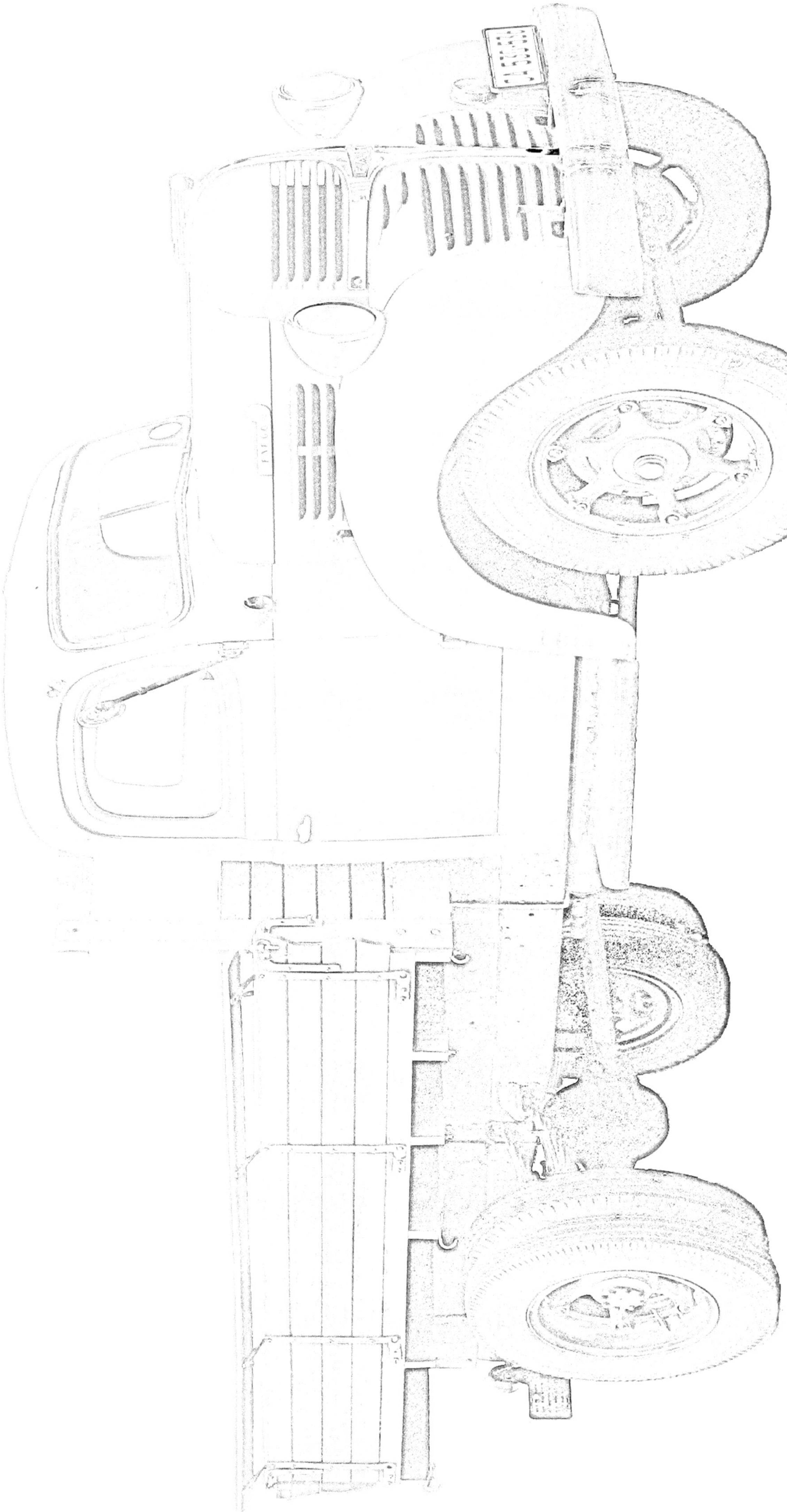

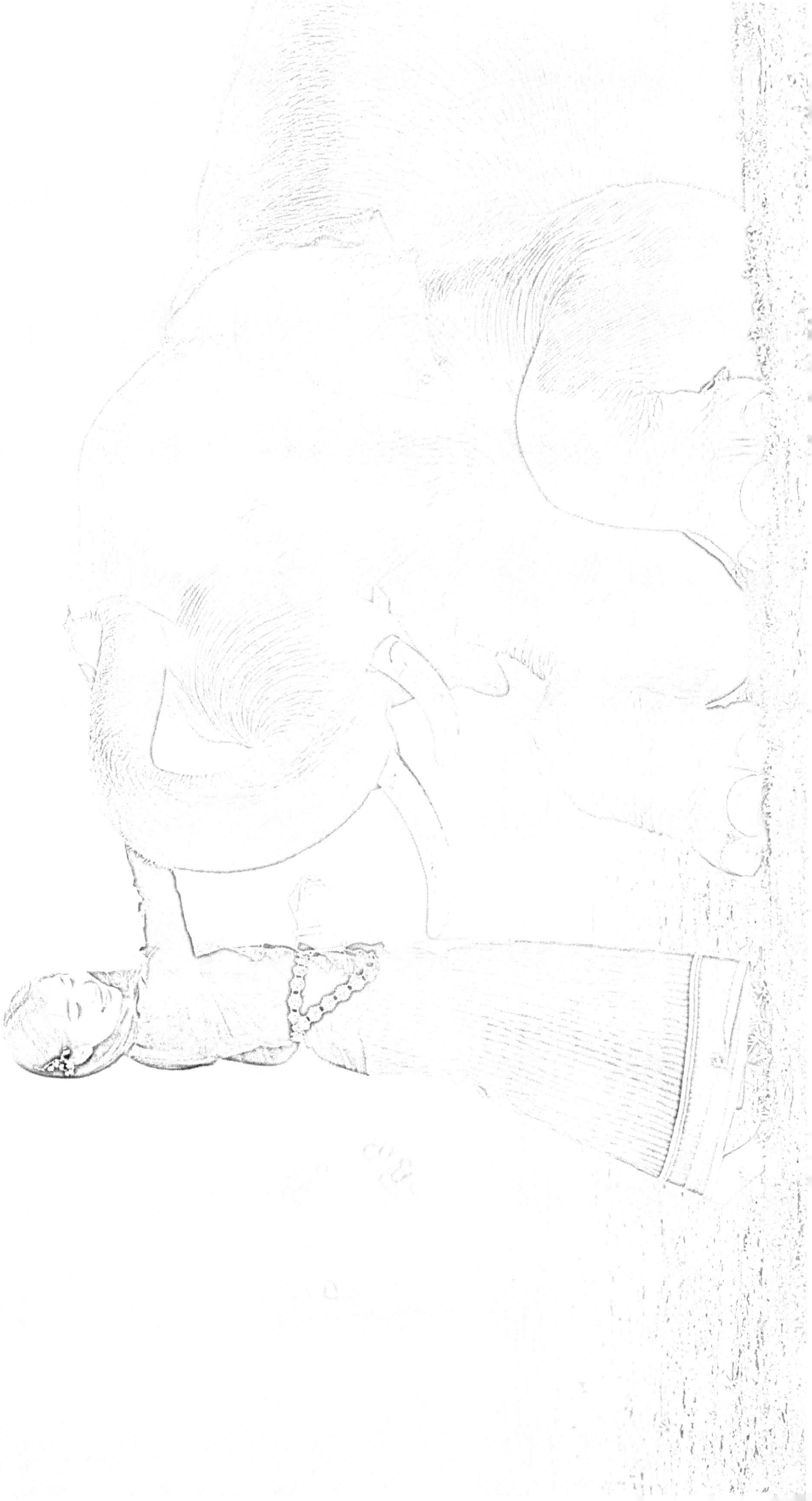

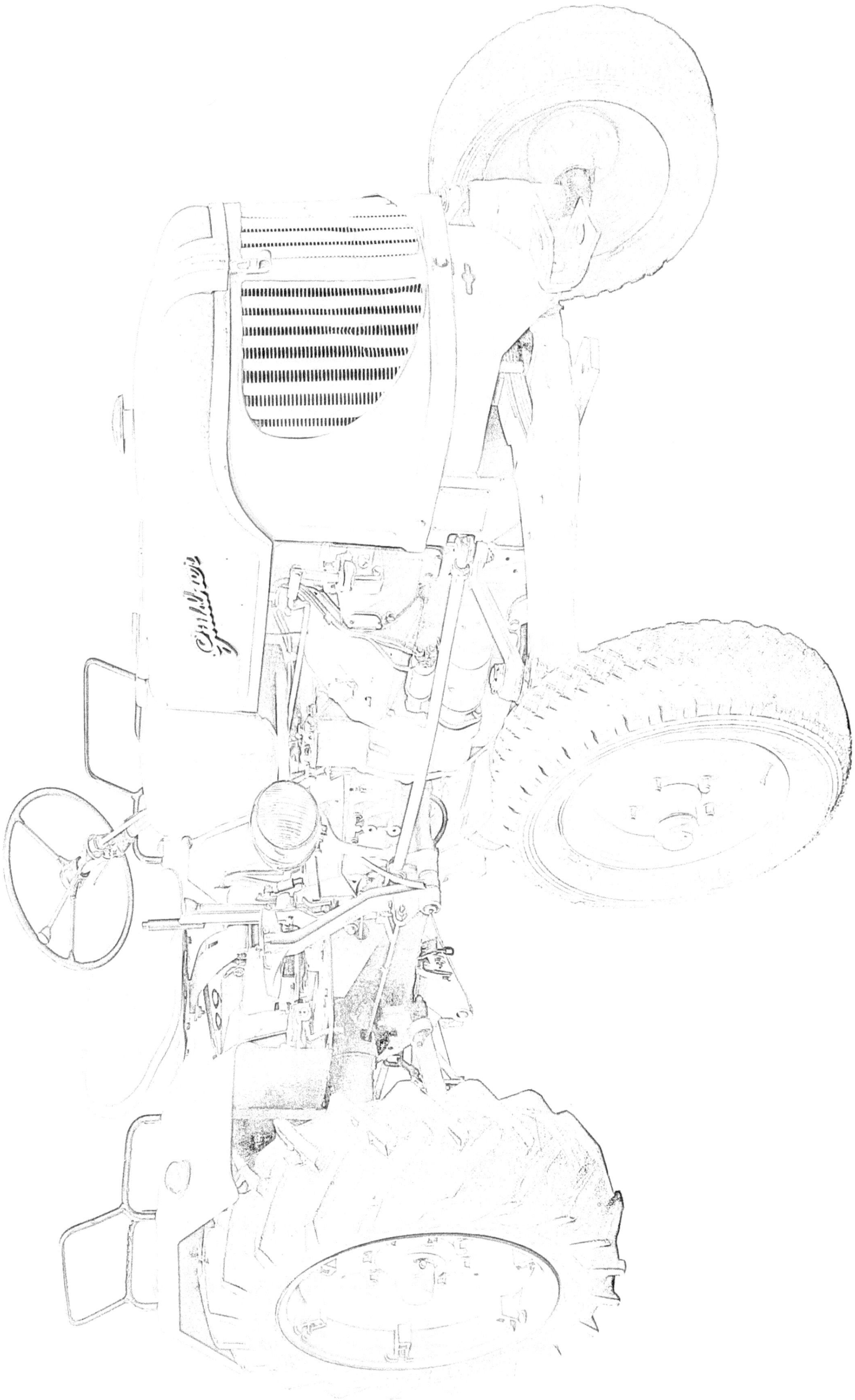

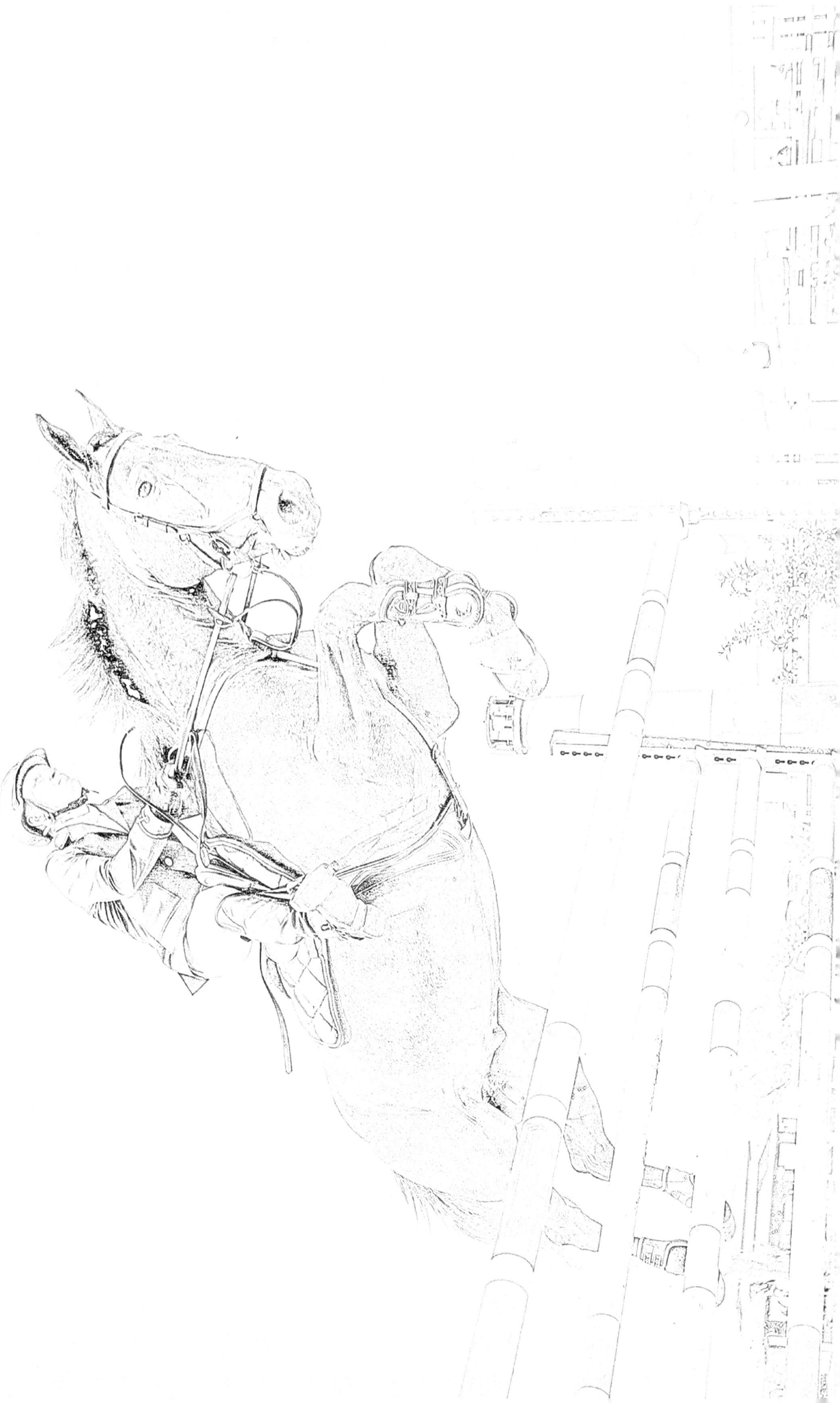

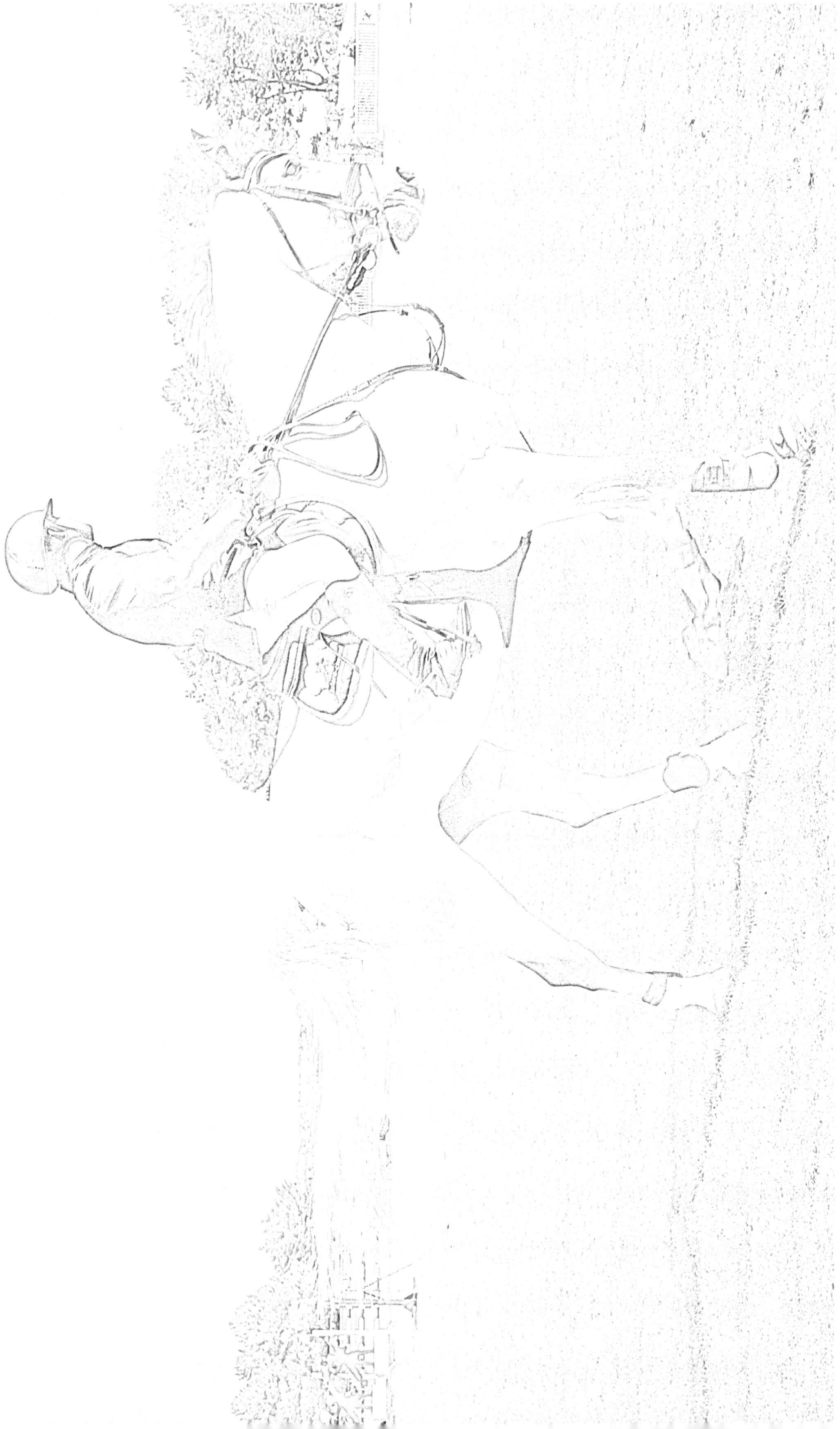

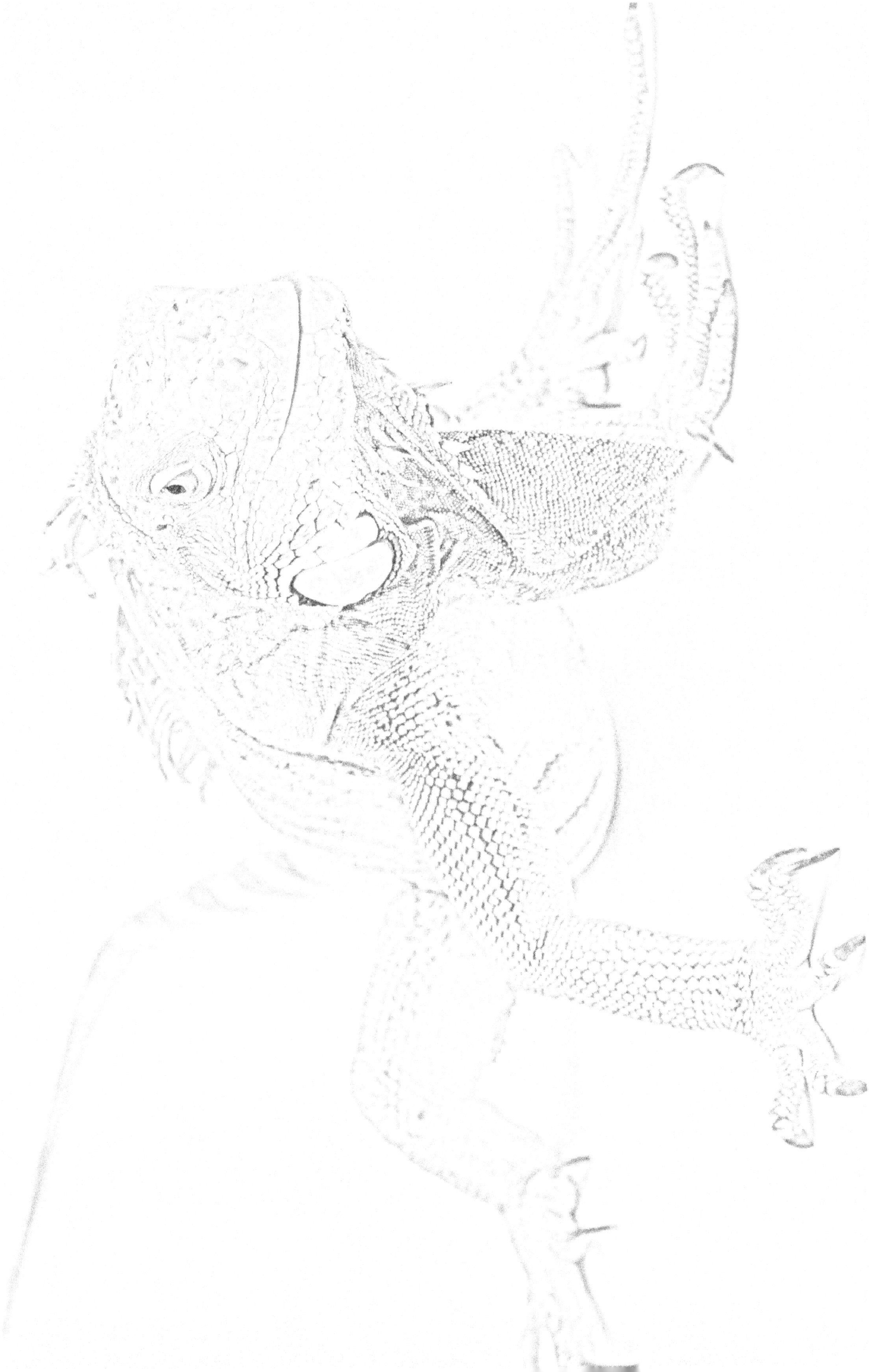

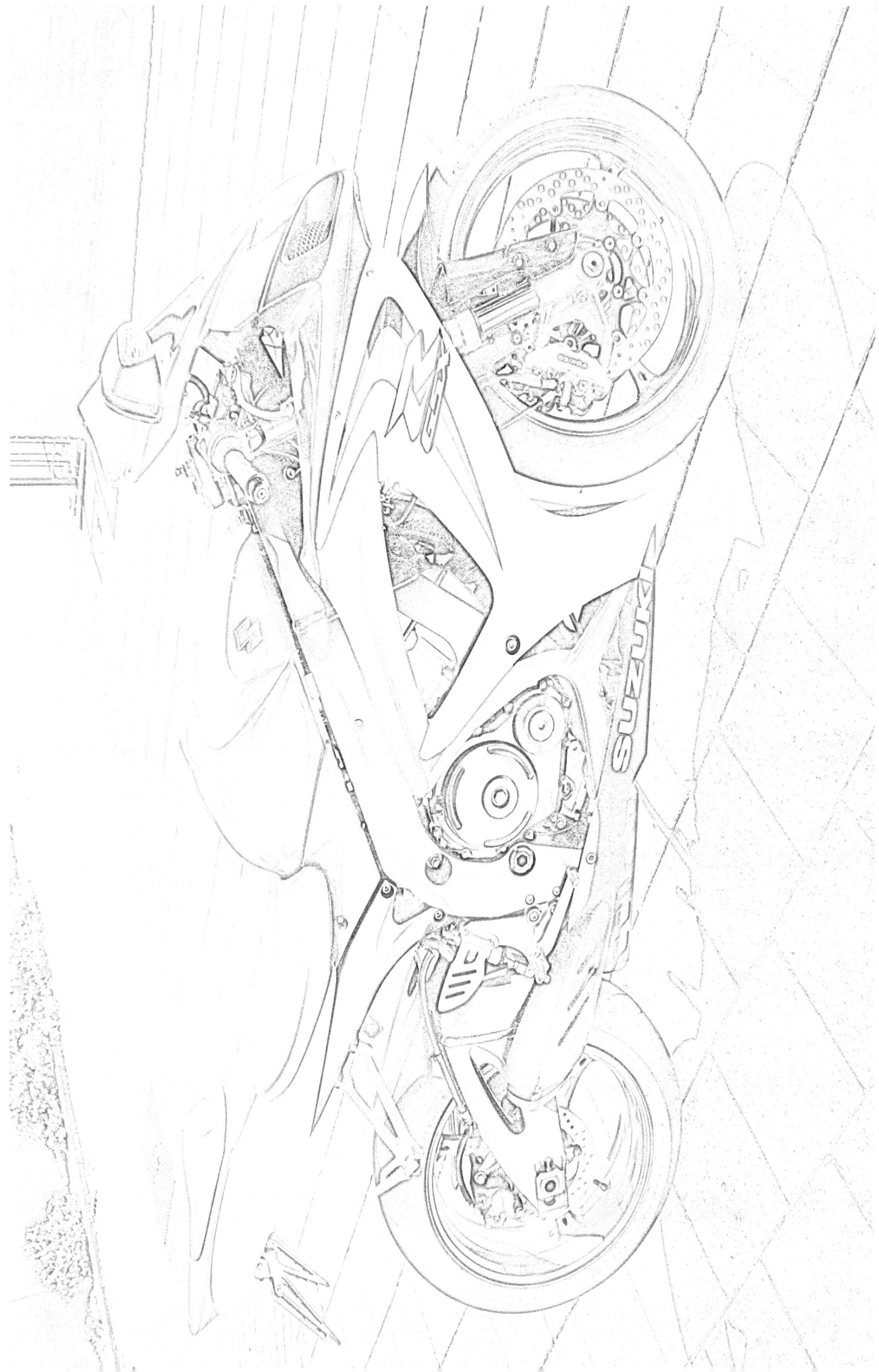
SUZUKI

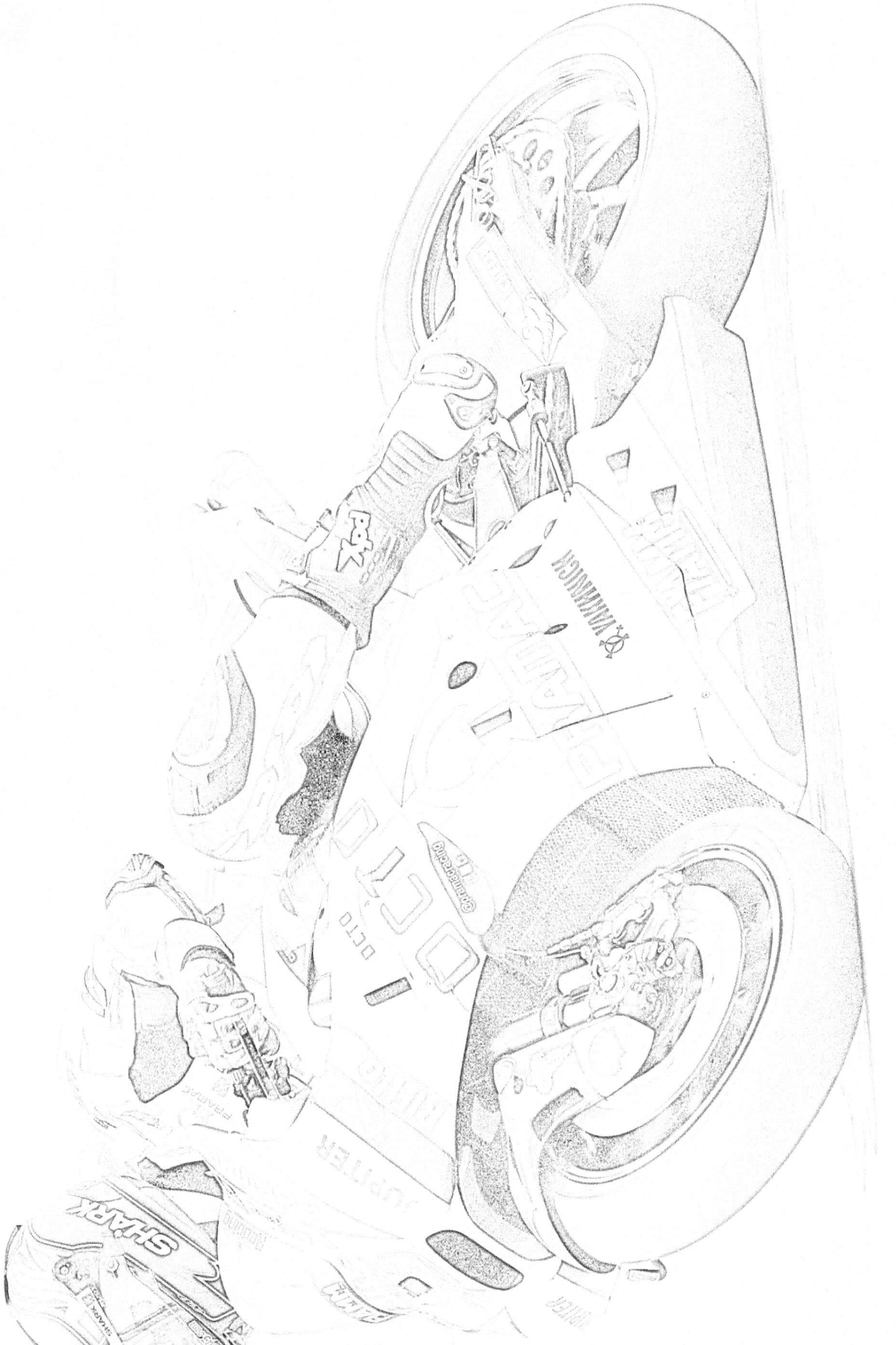
SHARK
JUPITER

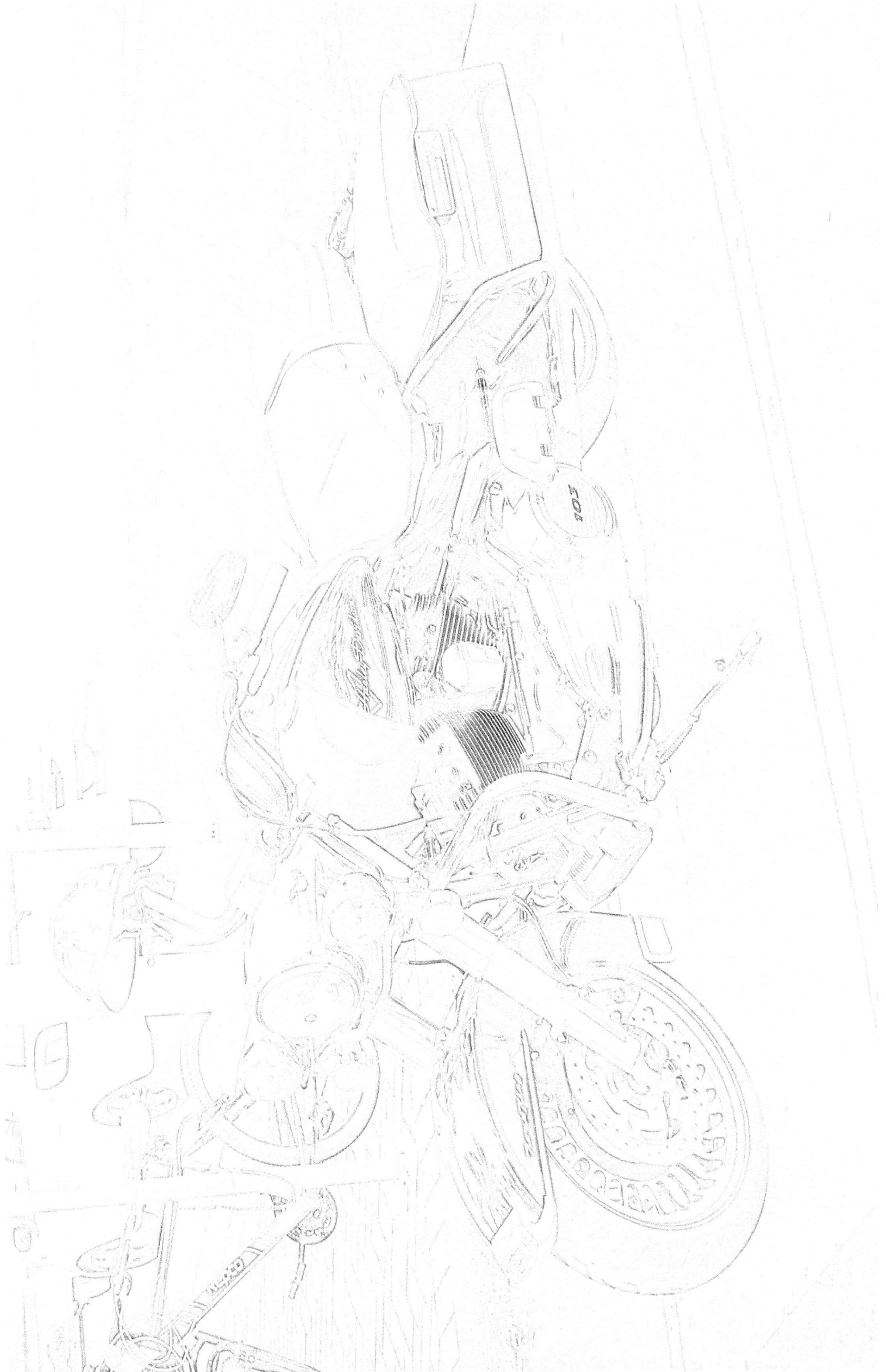
103

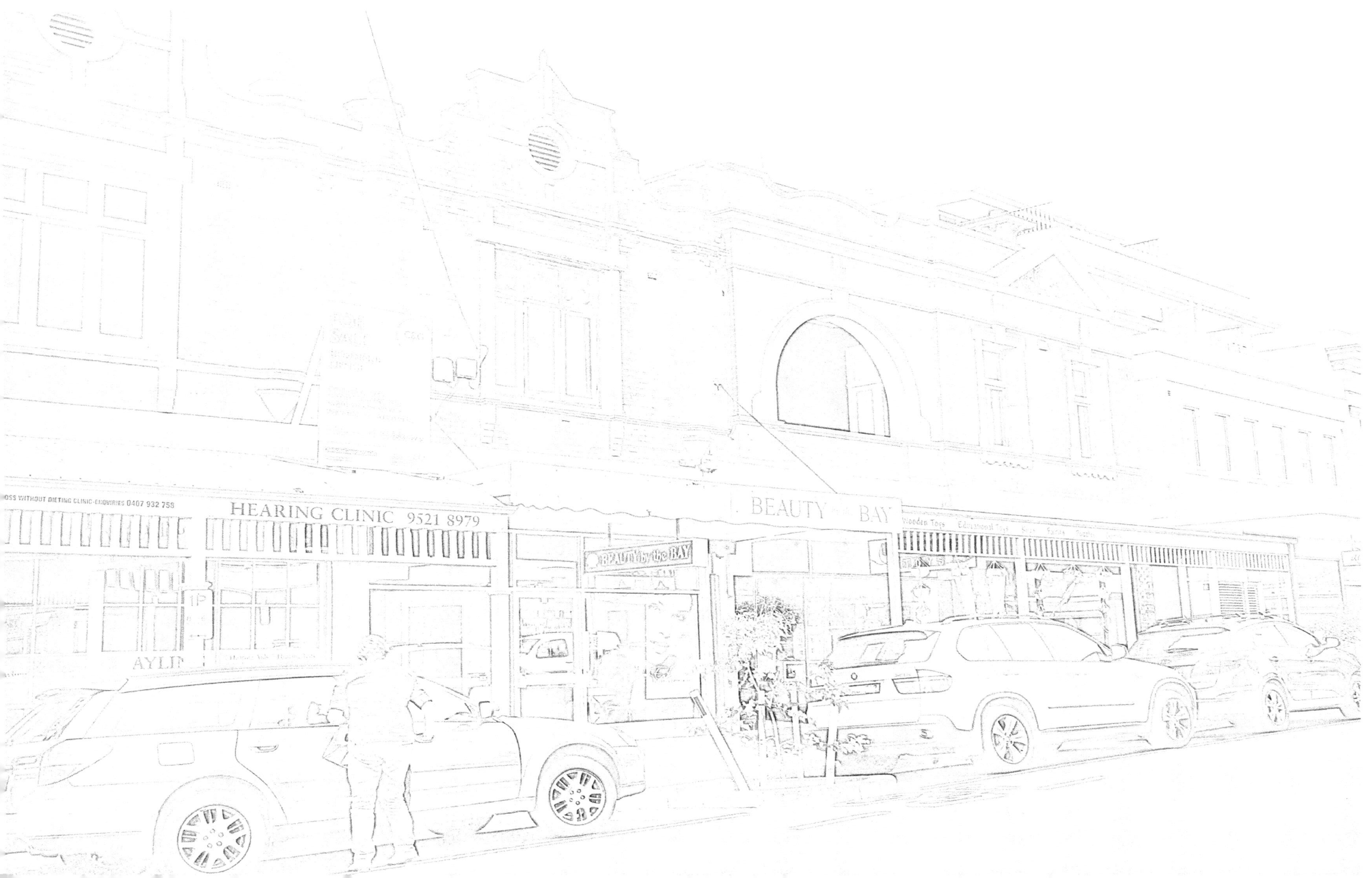
OSS WITHOUT DIETING CLINIC-ENQUIRIES 0407 932 758
HEARING CLINIC 9521 8979
BEAUTY BAY
BEAUTY by the BAY
Wooden Toys Educational Toys
1P
AYLI

MEAL & POT DEAL
19.50
SUNDAY ROAST
MONDAY CURRY
TUESDAY PARMA
WEDNESDAY PORTERHOUSE
OPEN 7 NIGHTS FROM 4 PM
SUNDAY FROM NOON
Op Shop
guitarsplus.com

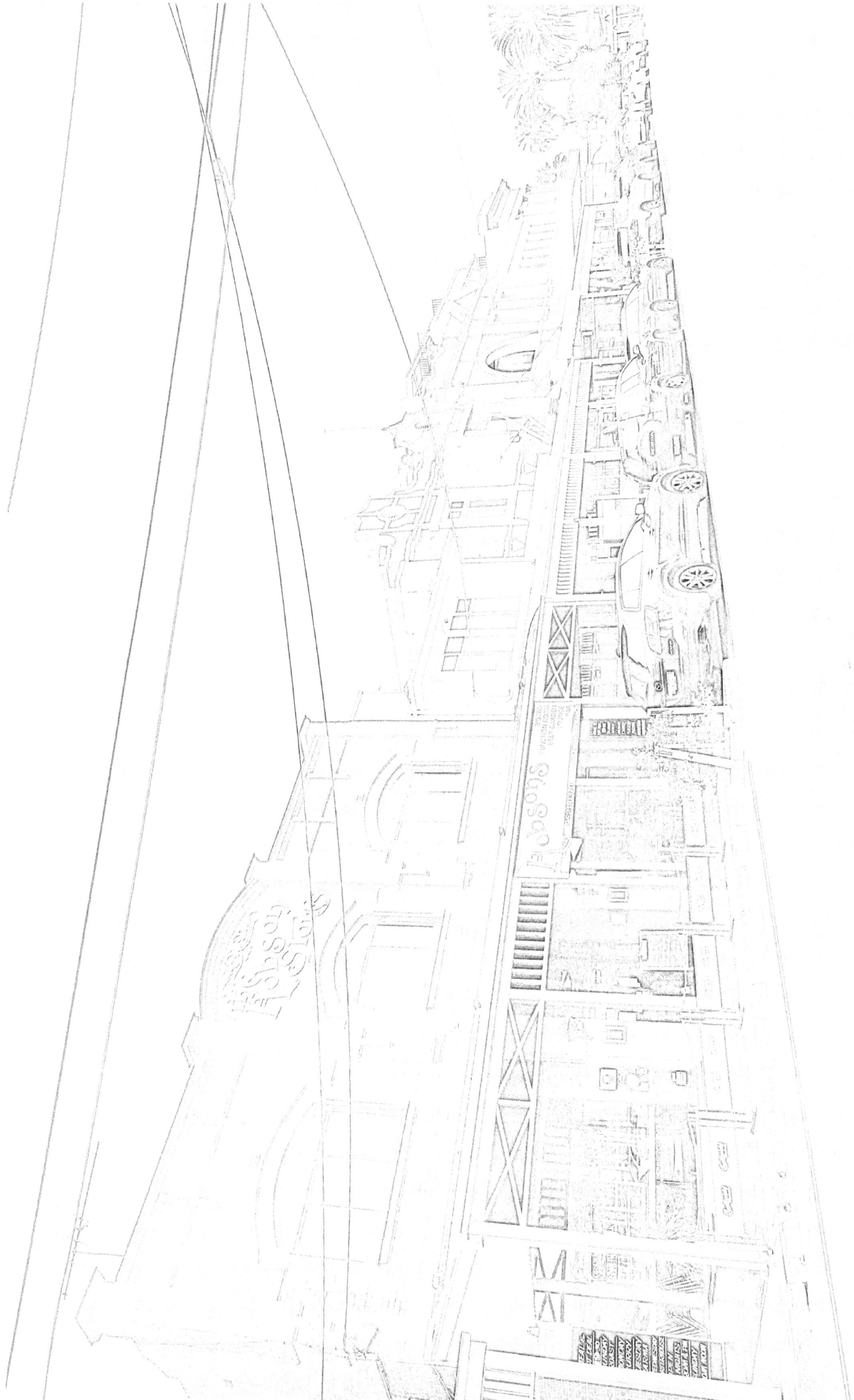

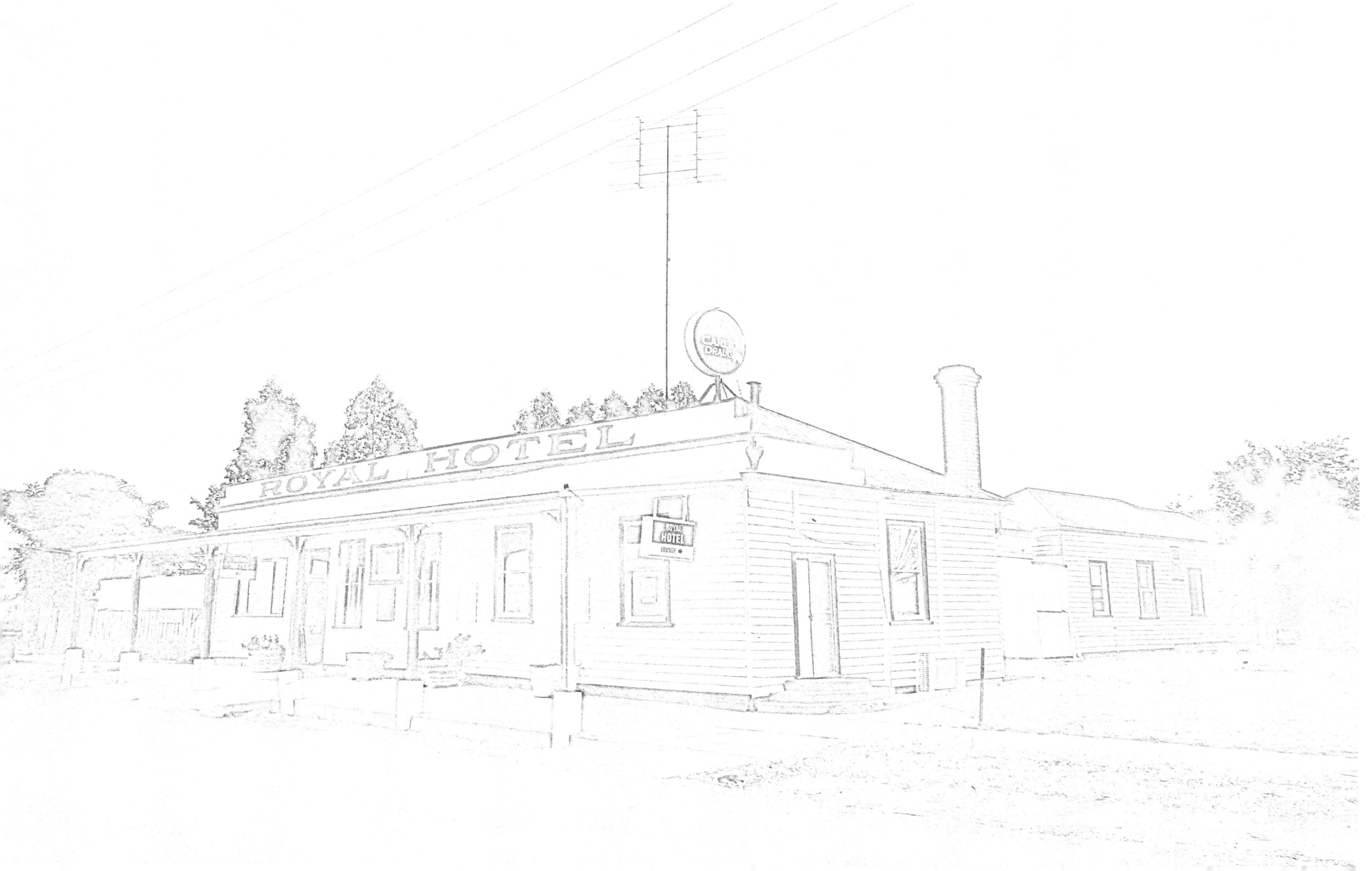
ROYAL HOTEL
ROYAL HOTEL LOUNGE

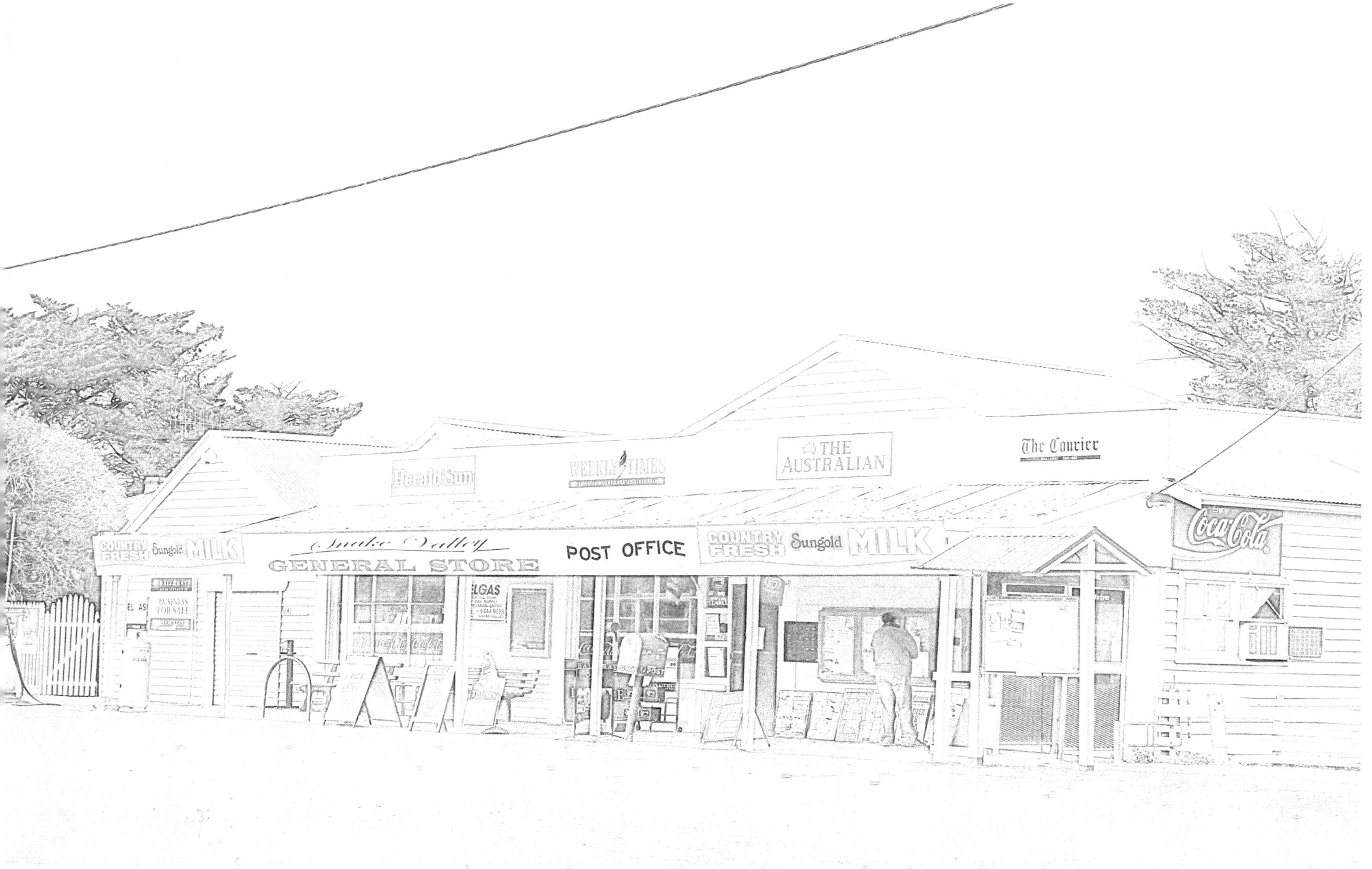
Herald Sun
WEEKLY TIMES
THE AUSTRALIAN
The Courier
Coca-Cola
COUNTRY FRESH
Sungold
MILK
Snake Valley
GENERAL STORE
POST OFFICE
COUNTRY FRESH
Sungold
MILK
BUSINESS FOR SALE
ELGAS

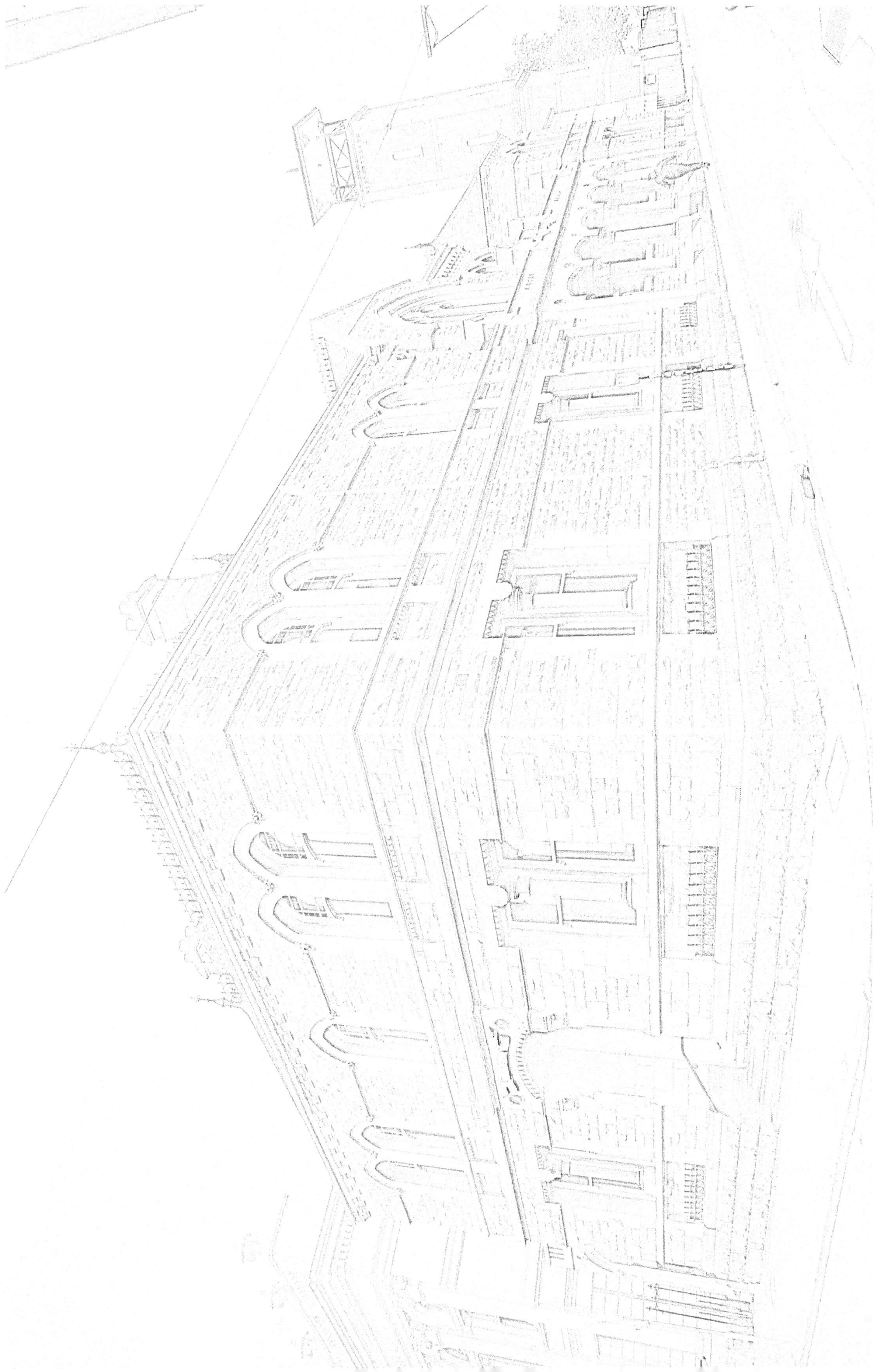

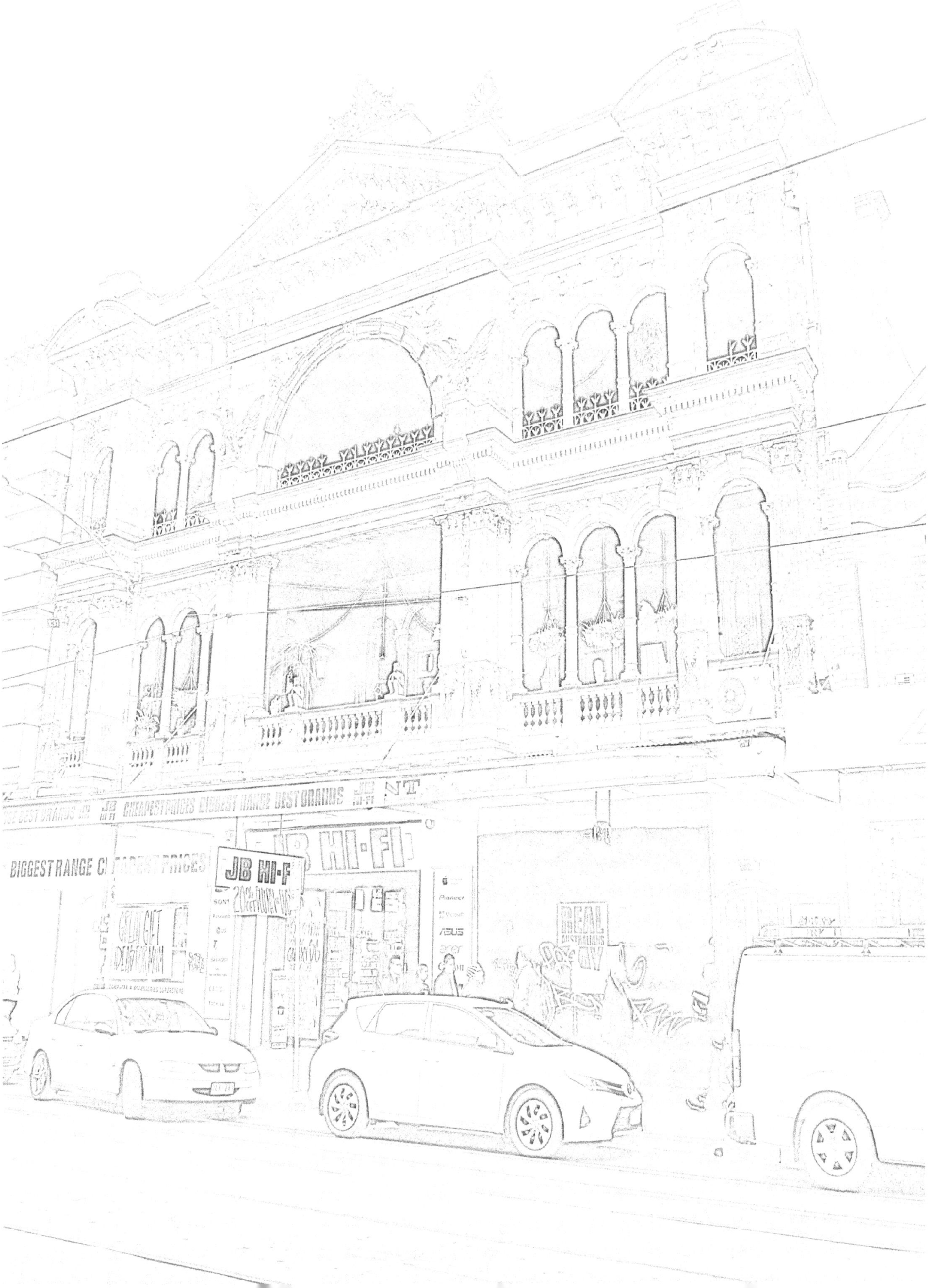
CHEAPEST PRICES BIGGEST RANGE BEST BRANDS
JB HI-FI
Pioneer
ASUS
acer

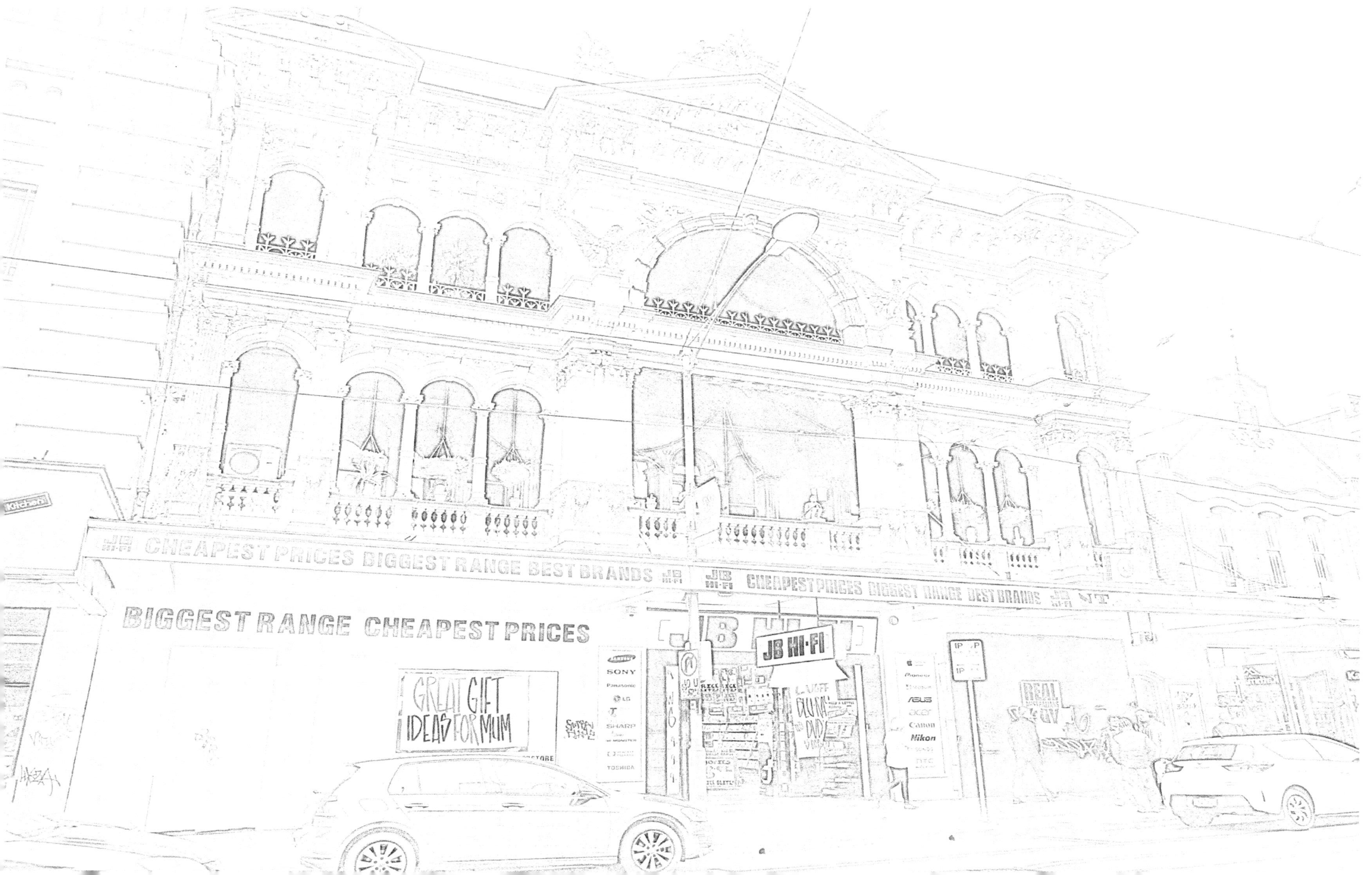
CHEAPEST PRICES BIGGEST RANGE BEST BRANDS
BIGGEST RANGE CHEAPEST PRICES
JB HI-FI
GREAT GIFT IDEAS FOR MUM
SONY
Panasonic
LG
SHARP
TOSHIBA
Pioneer
ASUS
acer
Canon
Nikon
REAL

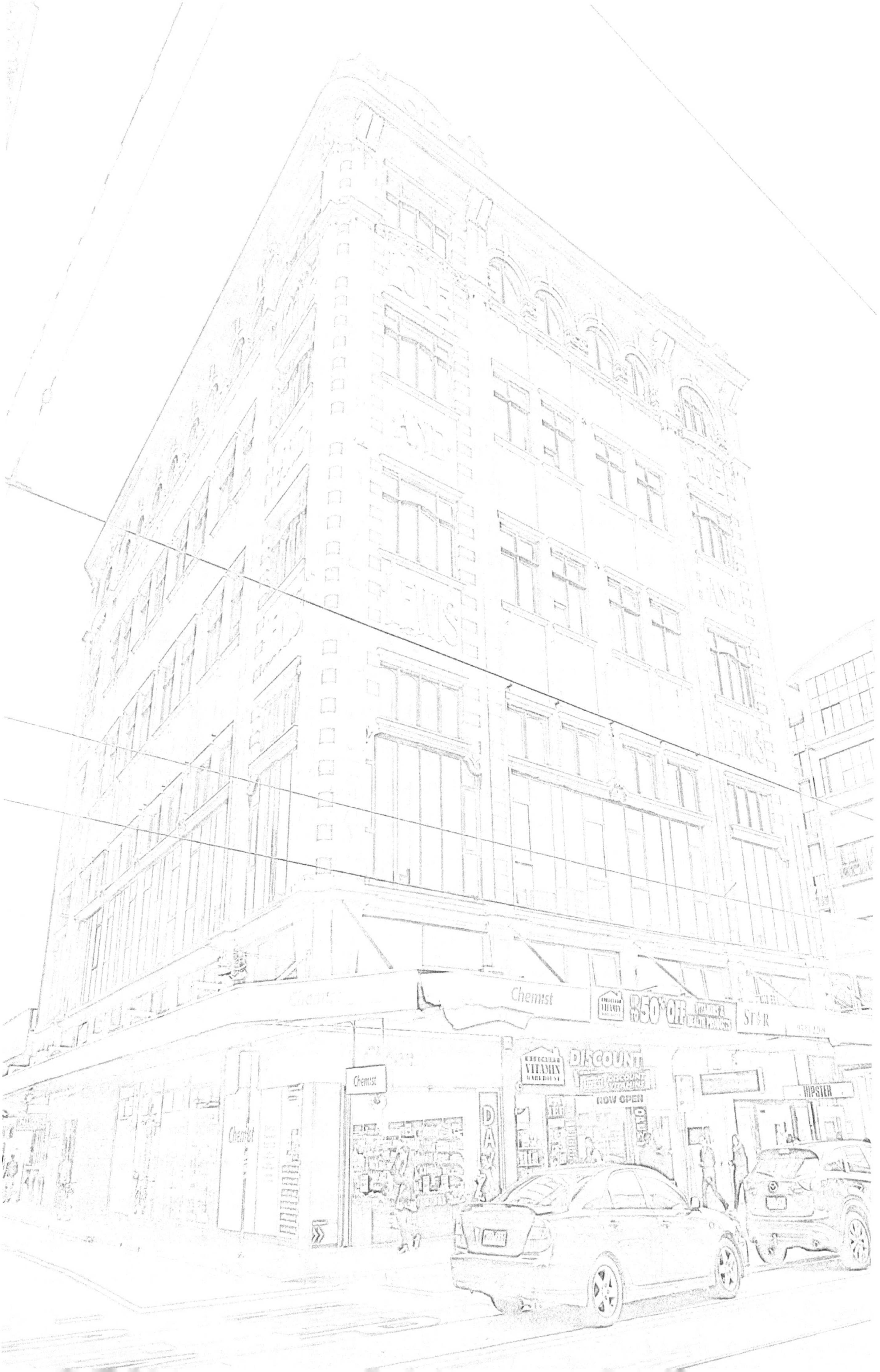
Chemist
Chemist
DISCOUNT
NOW OPEN
HIPSTER

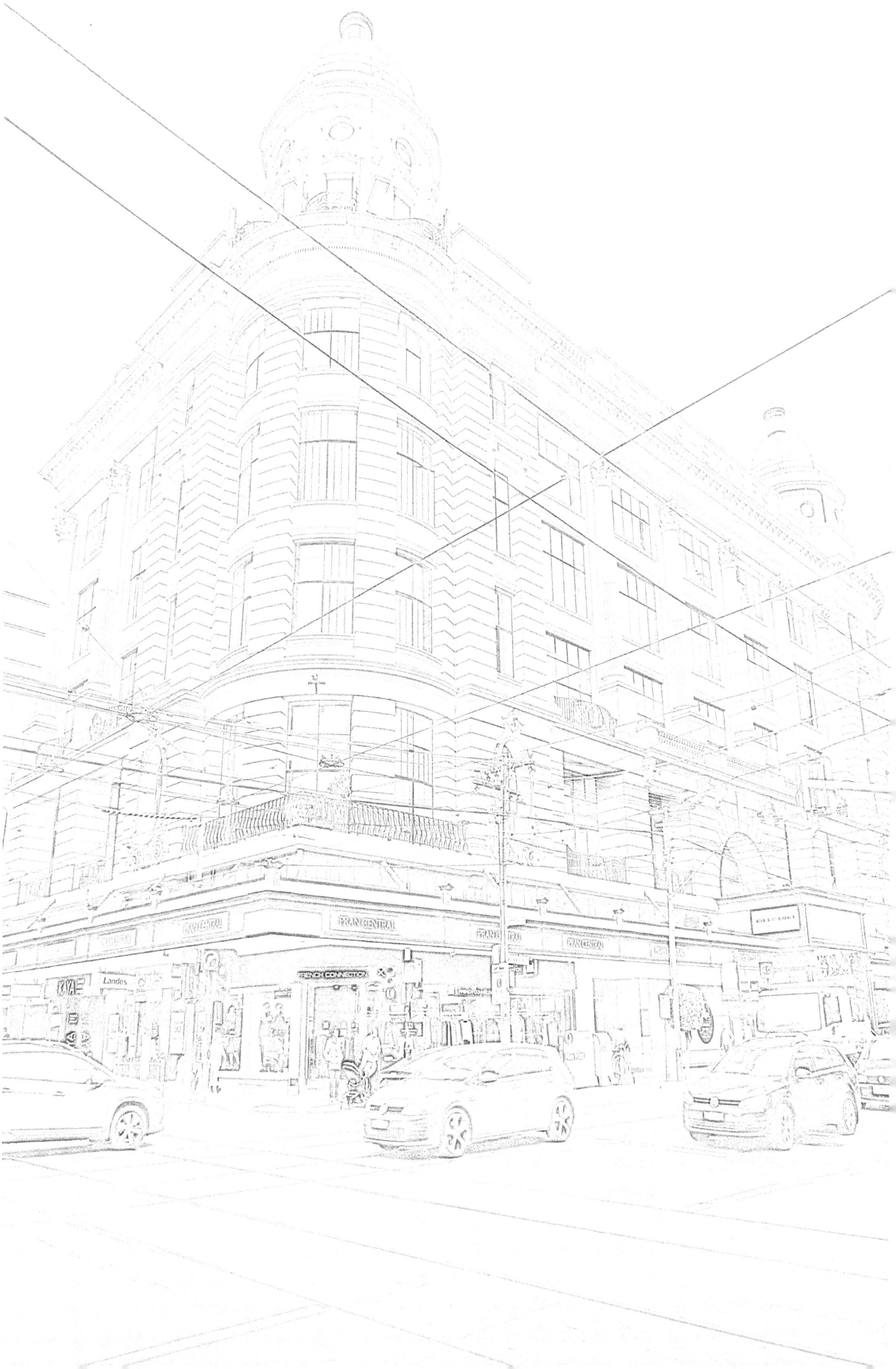
PRAN CENTRAL
FRENCH CONNECTION
Landes

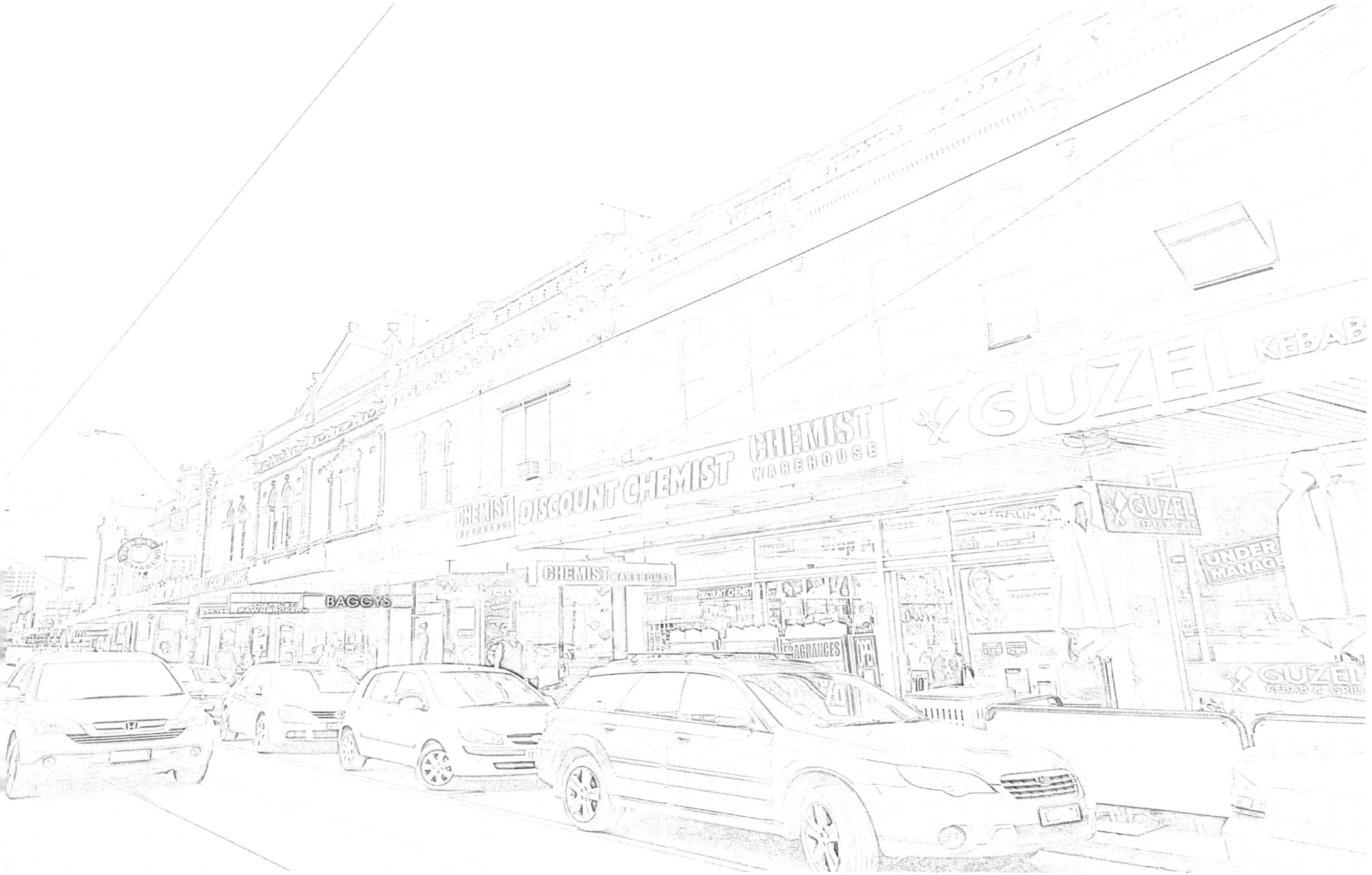
GUZEL KEBAB
CHEMIST WAREHOUSE
DISCOUNT CHEMIST
CHEMIST WAREHOUSE
GUZEL KEBAB & GRILL
BAGGYS
CHAPEL ST PAWNBROKER
FRAGRANCES

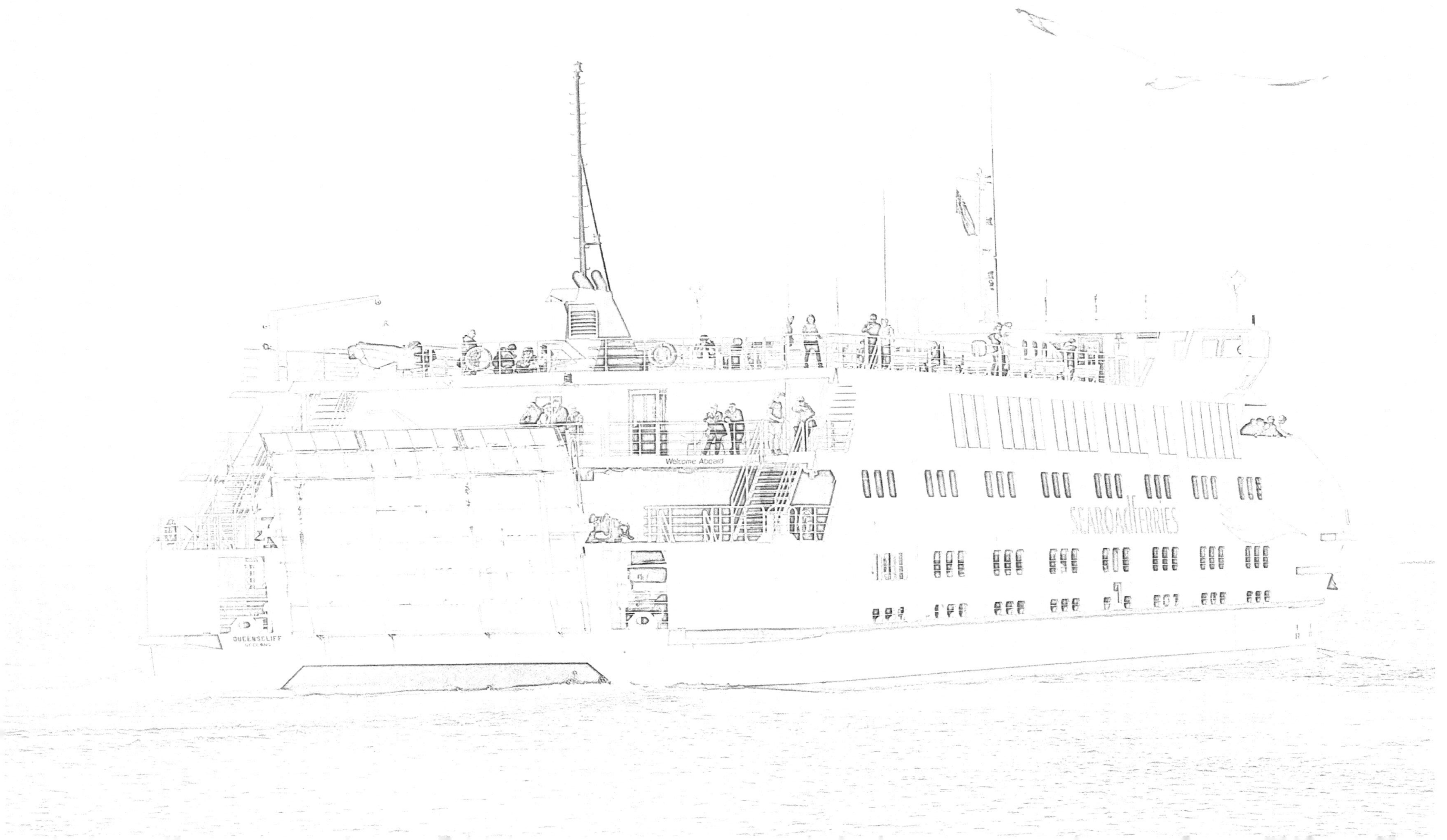
Welcome Aboard
SEAROADFERRIES
QUEENSCLIFF

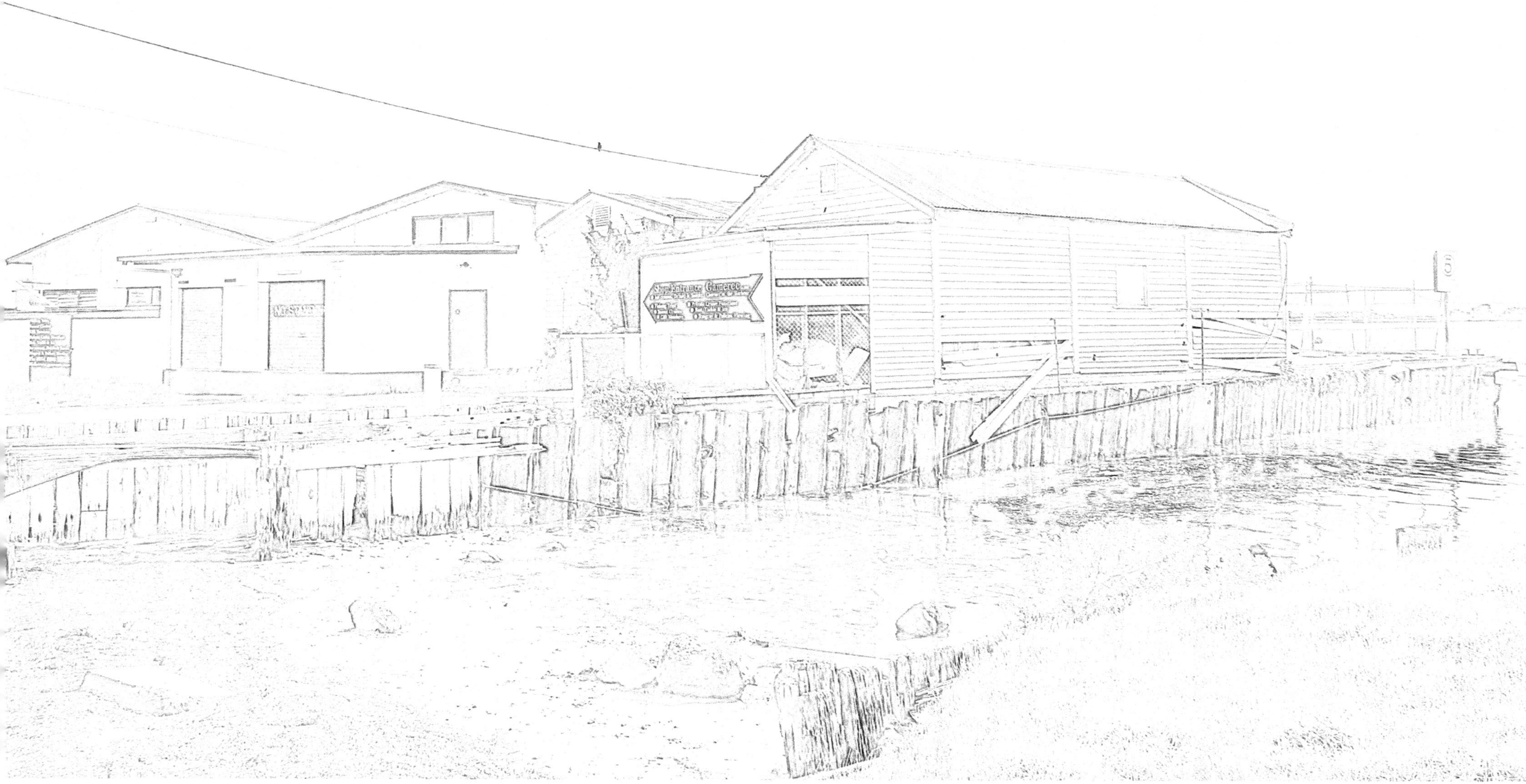

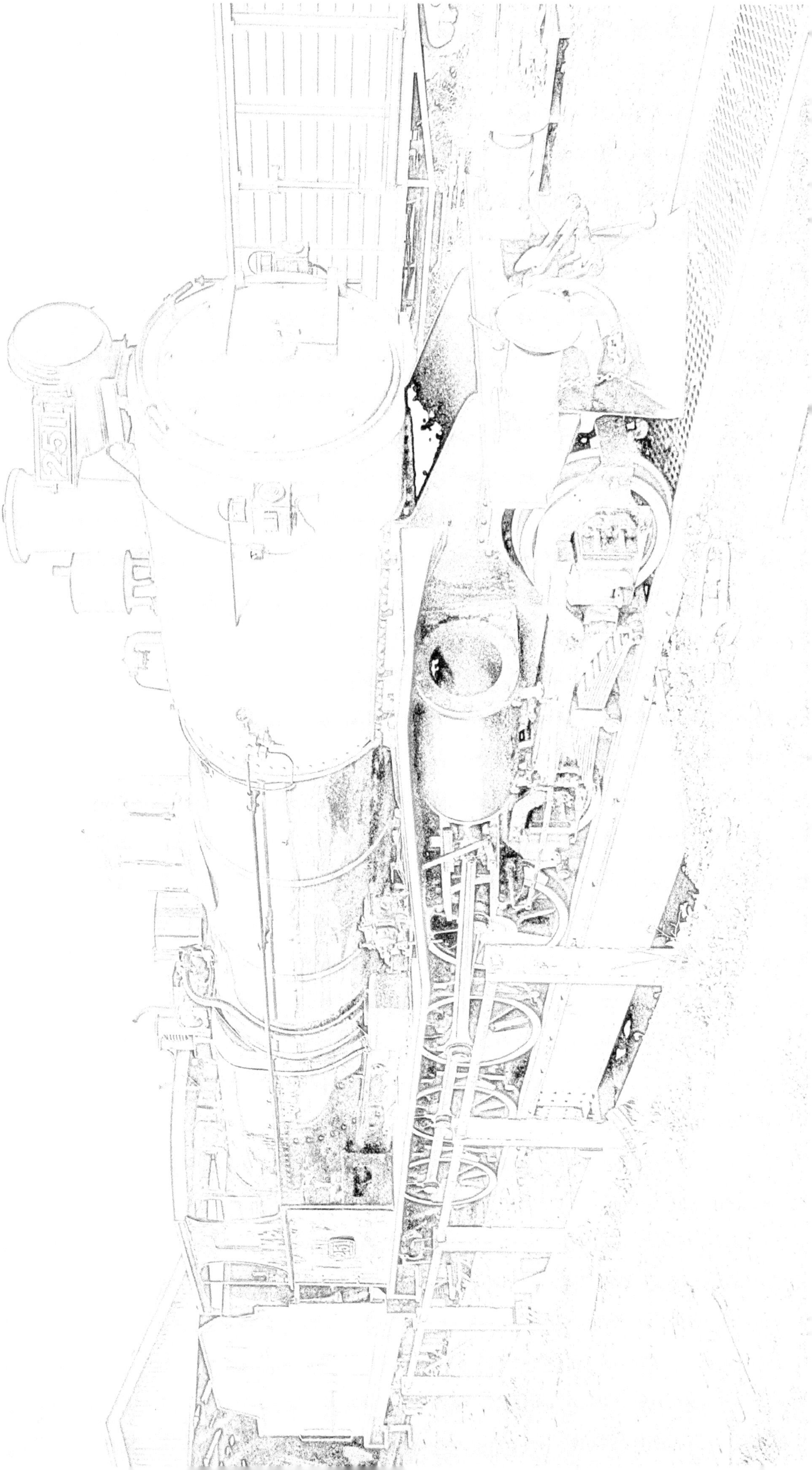
251

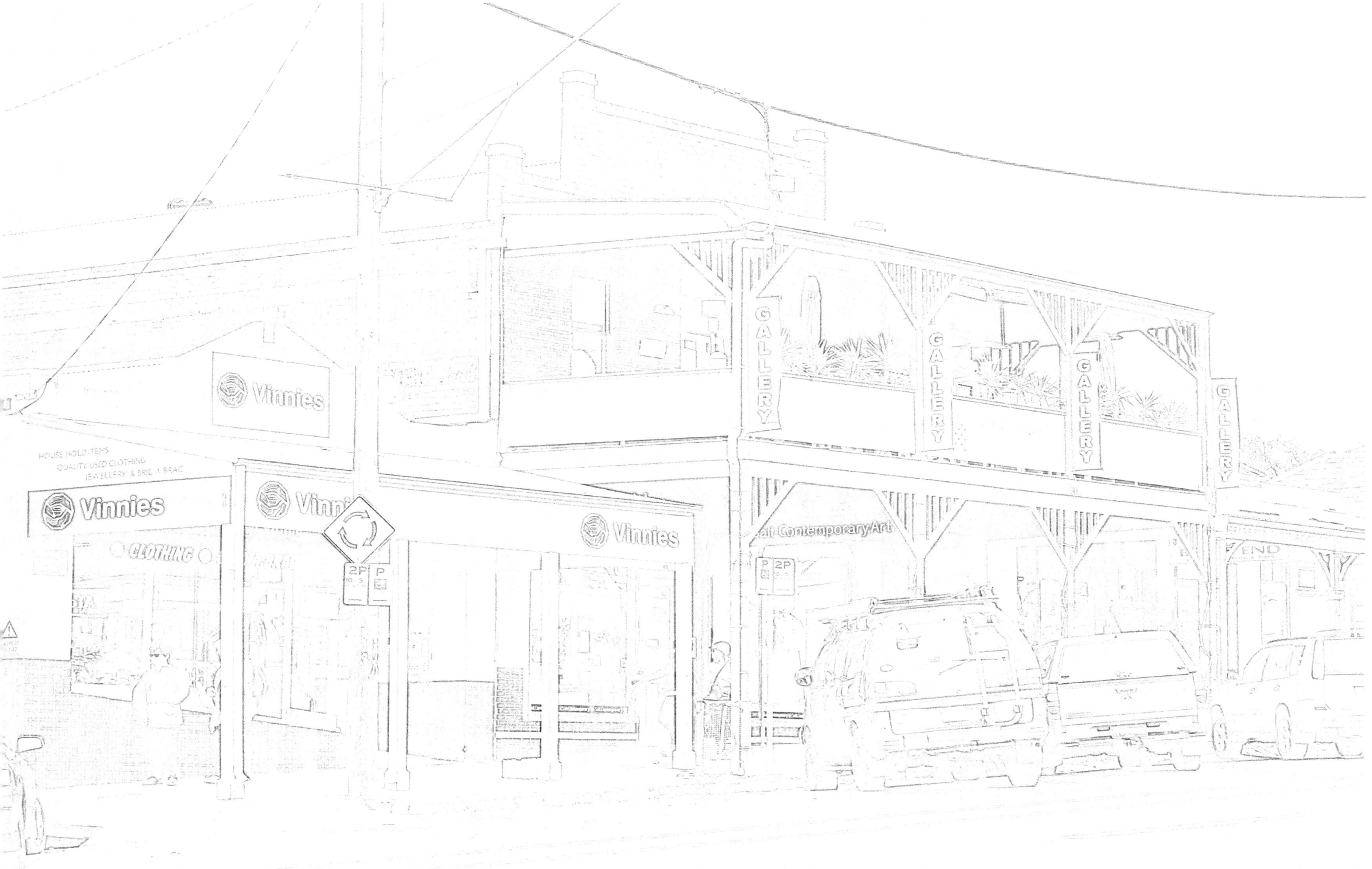

Vinnies
HOUSE HOLD ITEMS
QUALITY USED CLOTHING
JEWELLERY & BRIC A BRAC
Vinnies
CLOTHING
Vinnies
2P
P
Vinnies
GALLERY
GALLERY
GALLERY
GALLERY
Contemporary Art
P
2P
END

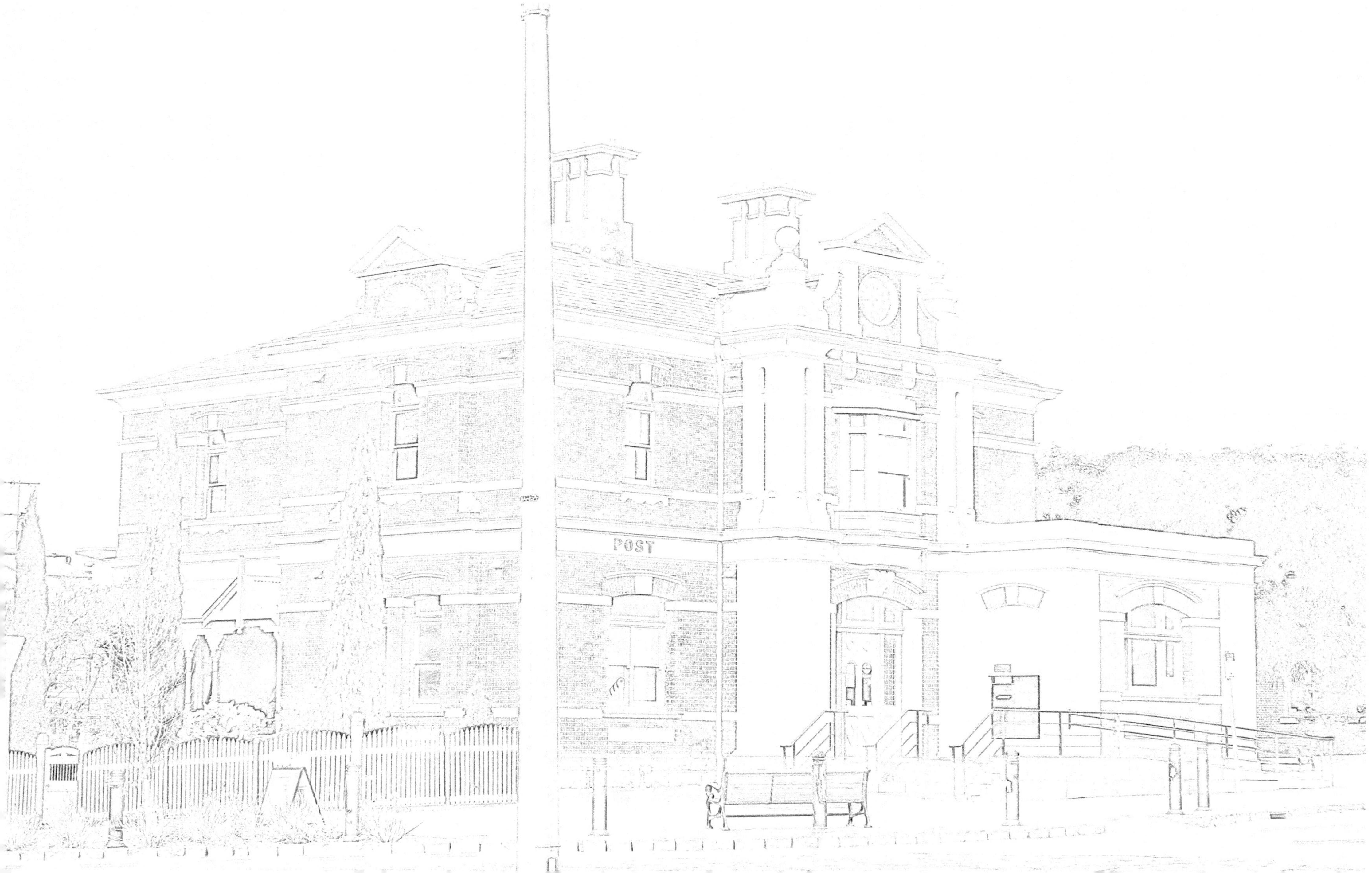
POST

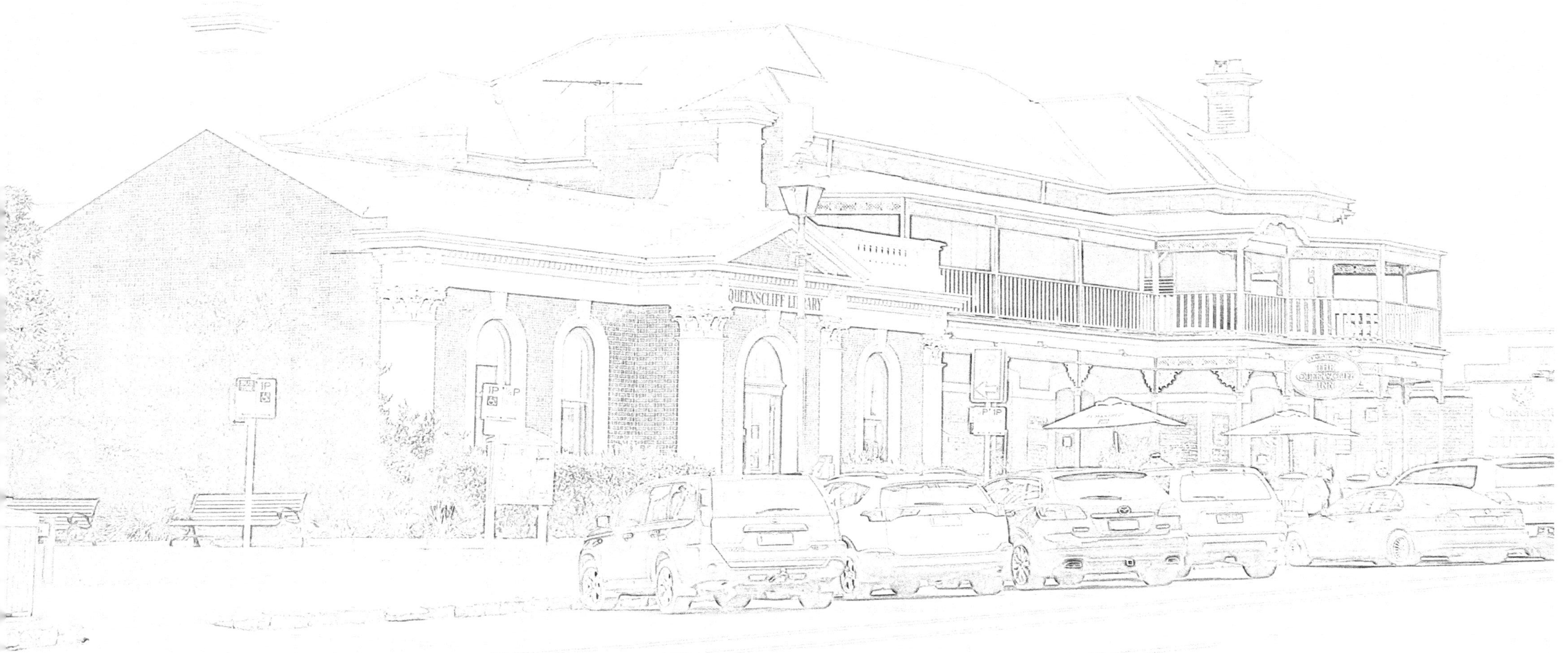
QUEENSCLIFF
THE
INN
1P

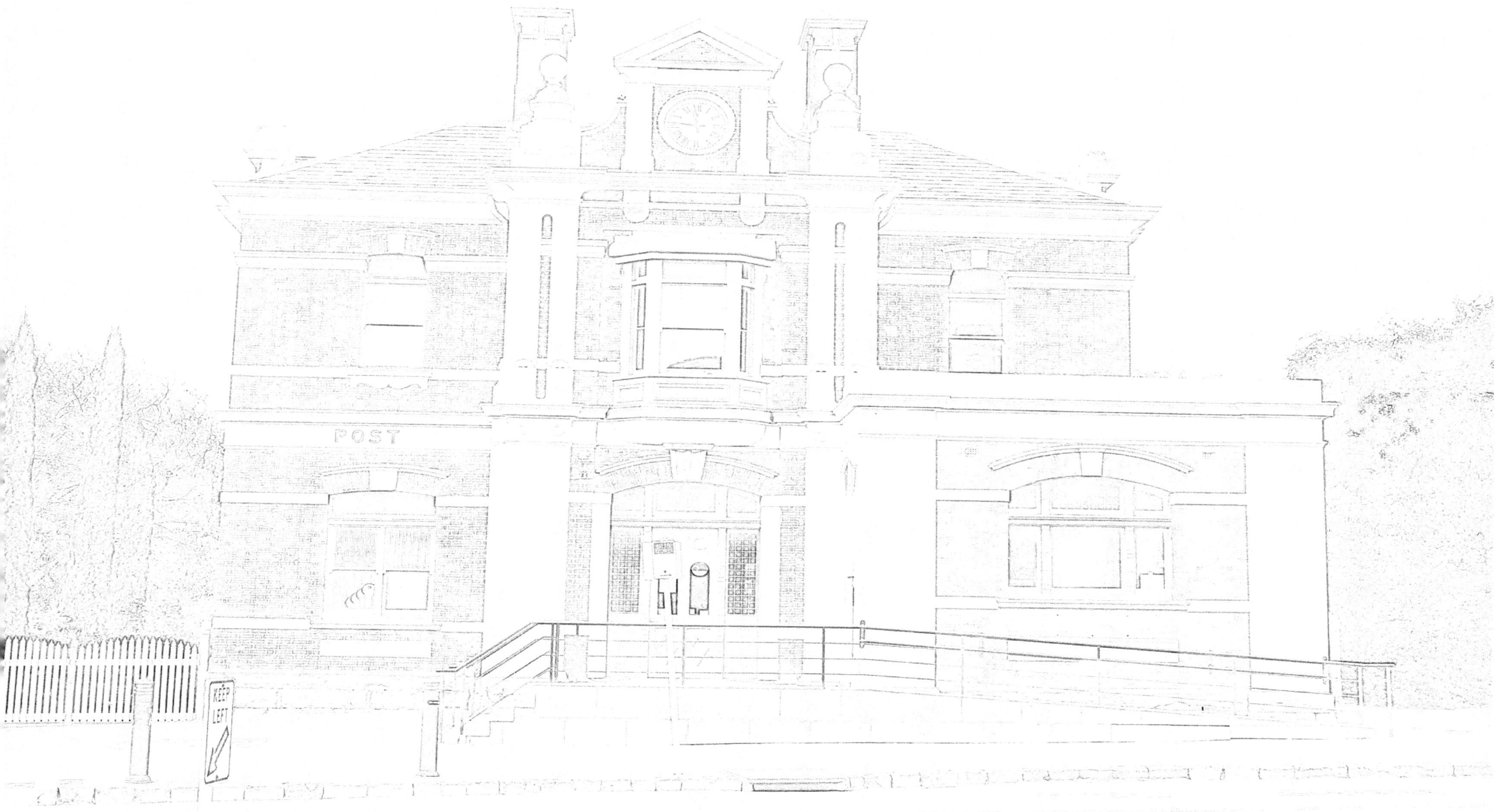
POST
KEEP LEFT

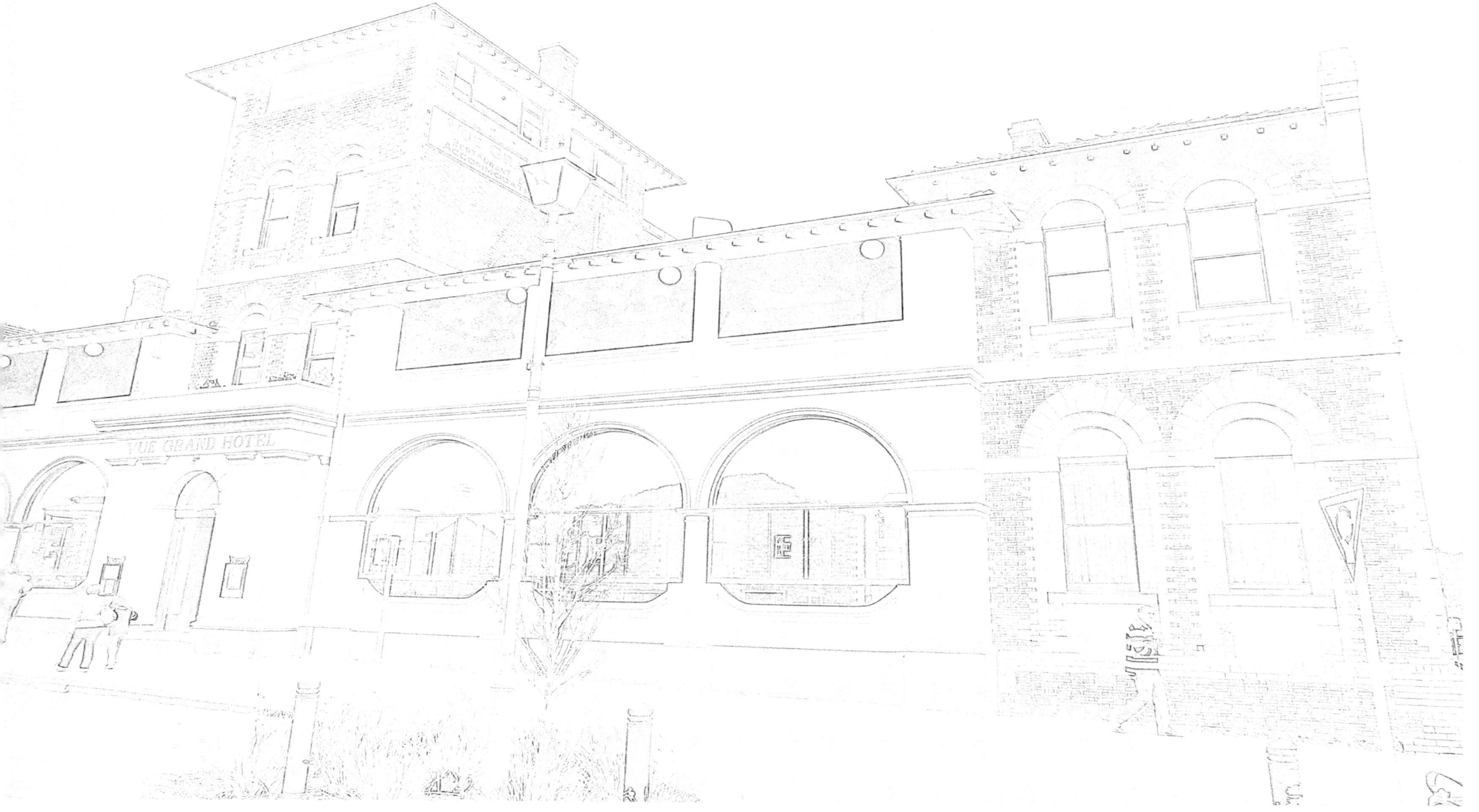
VUE GRAND HOTEL

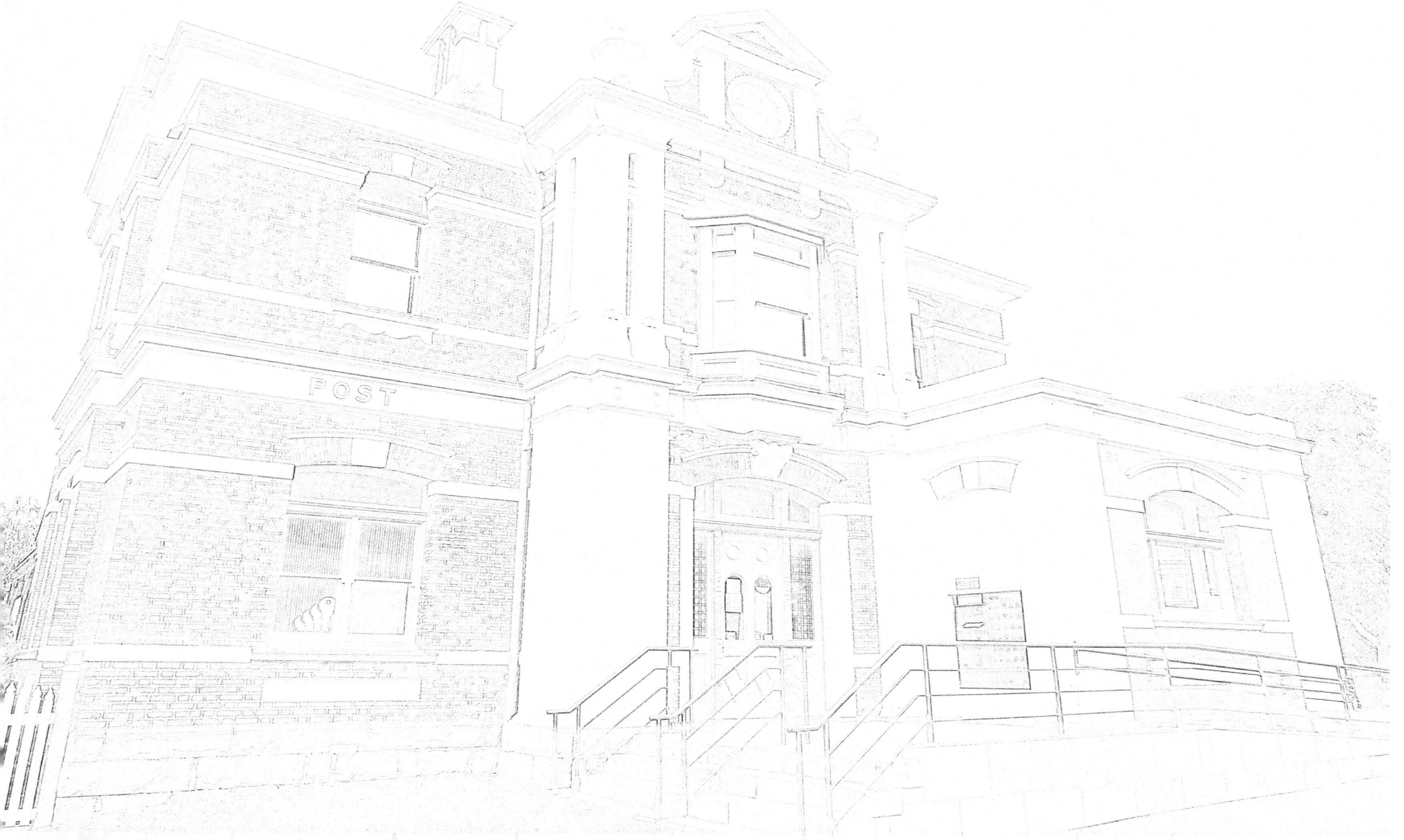
POST

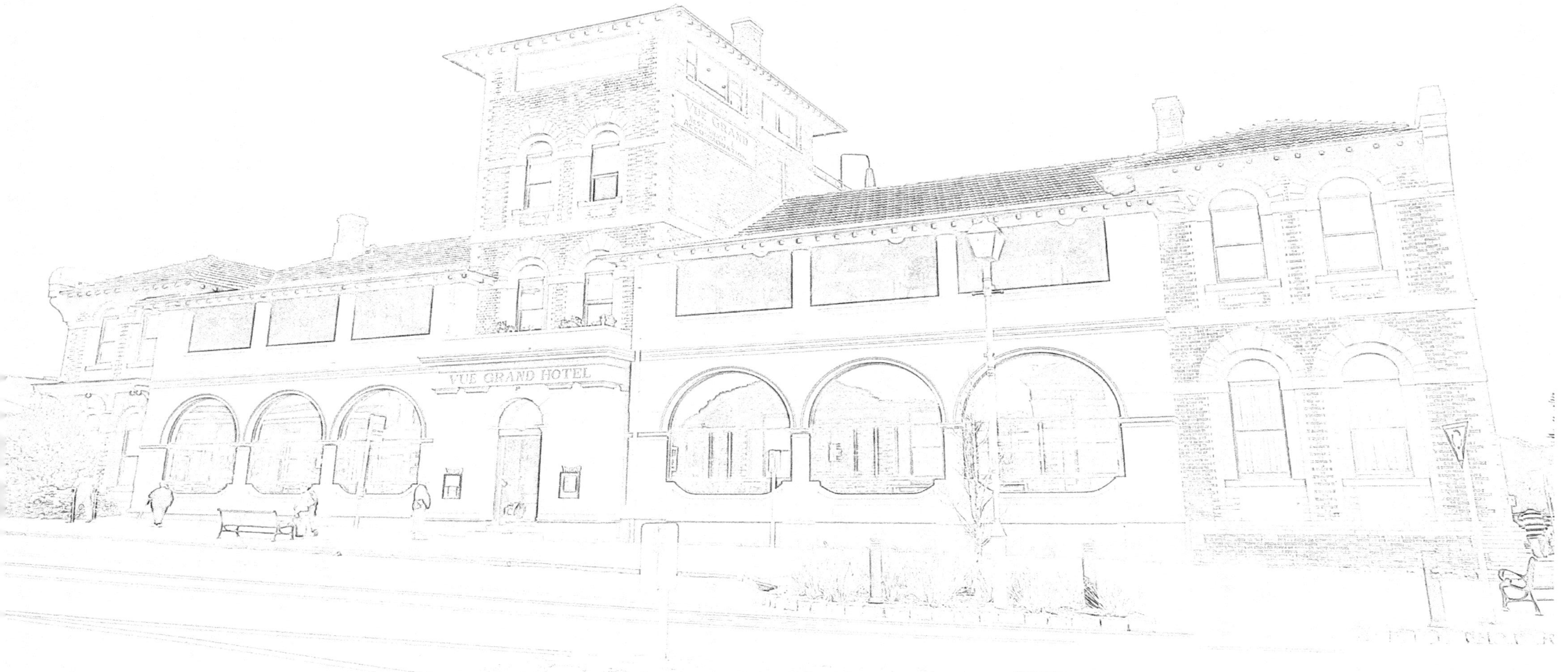
VUE GRAND HOTEL

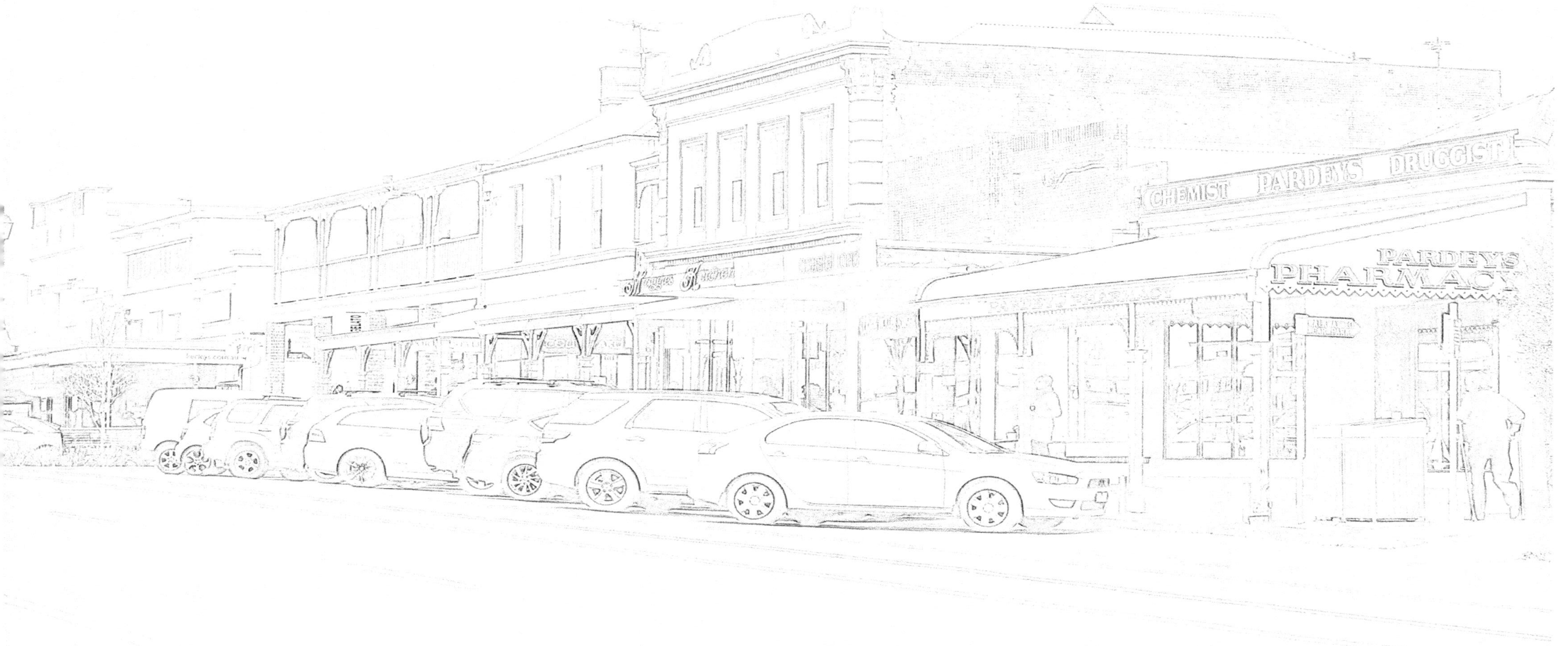
CHEMIST PARDEYS DRUGGIST
PARDEYS
PHARMACY

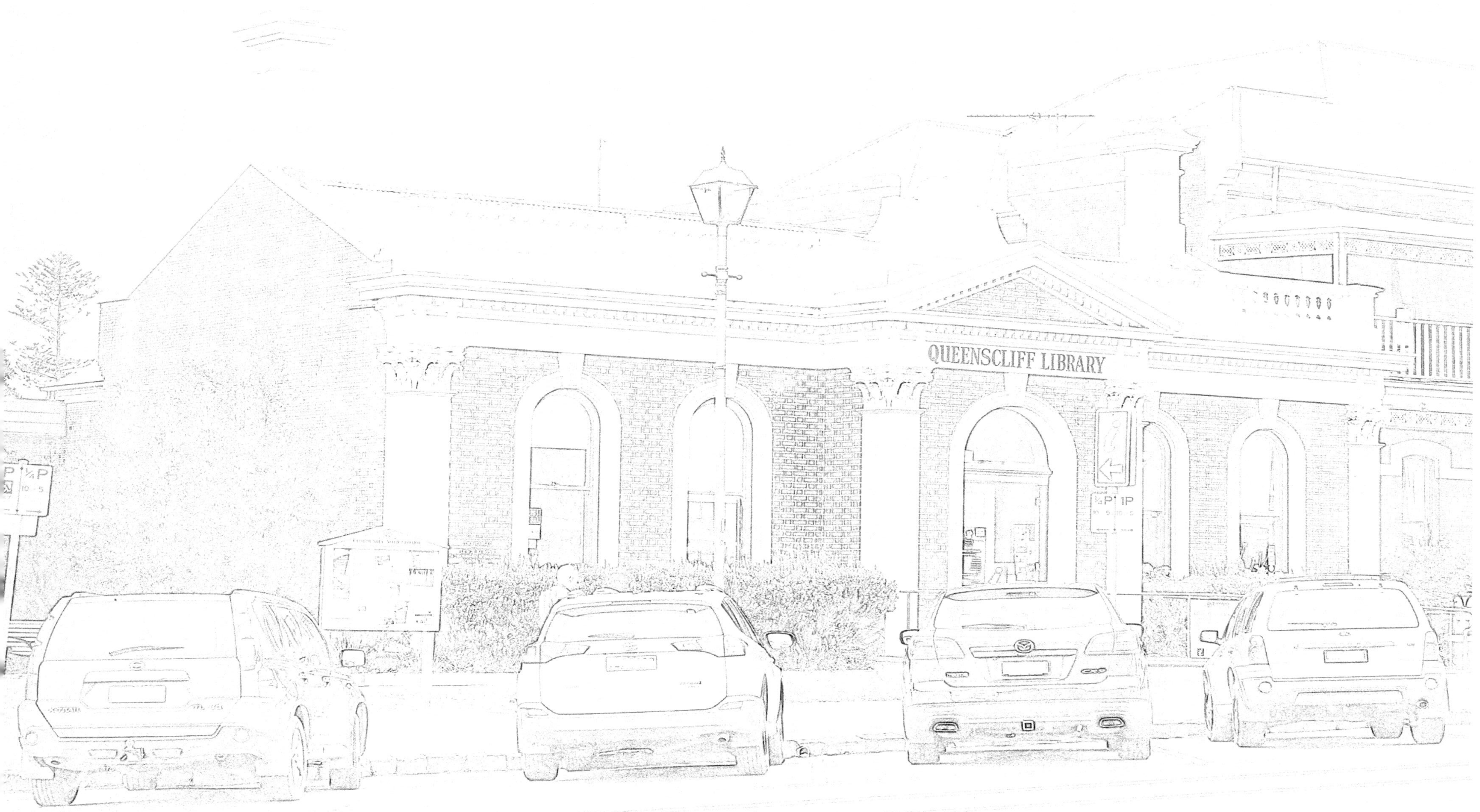
QUEENSCLIFF LIBRARY
¼P
1P

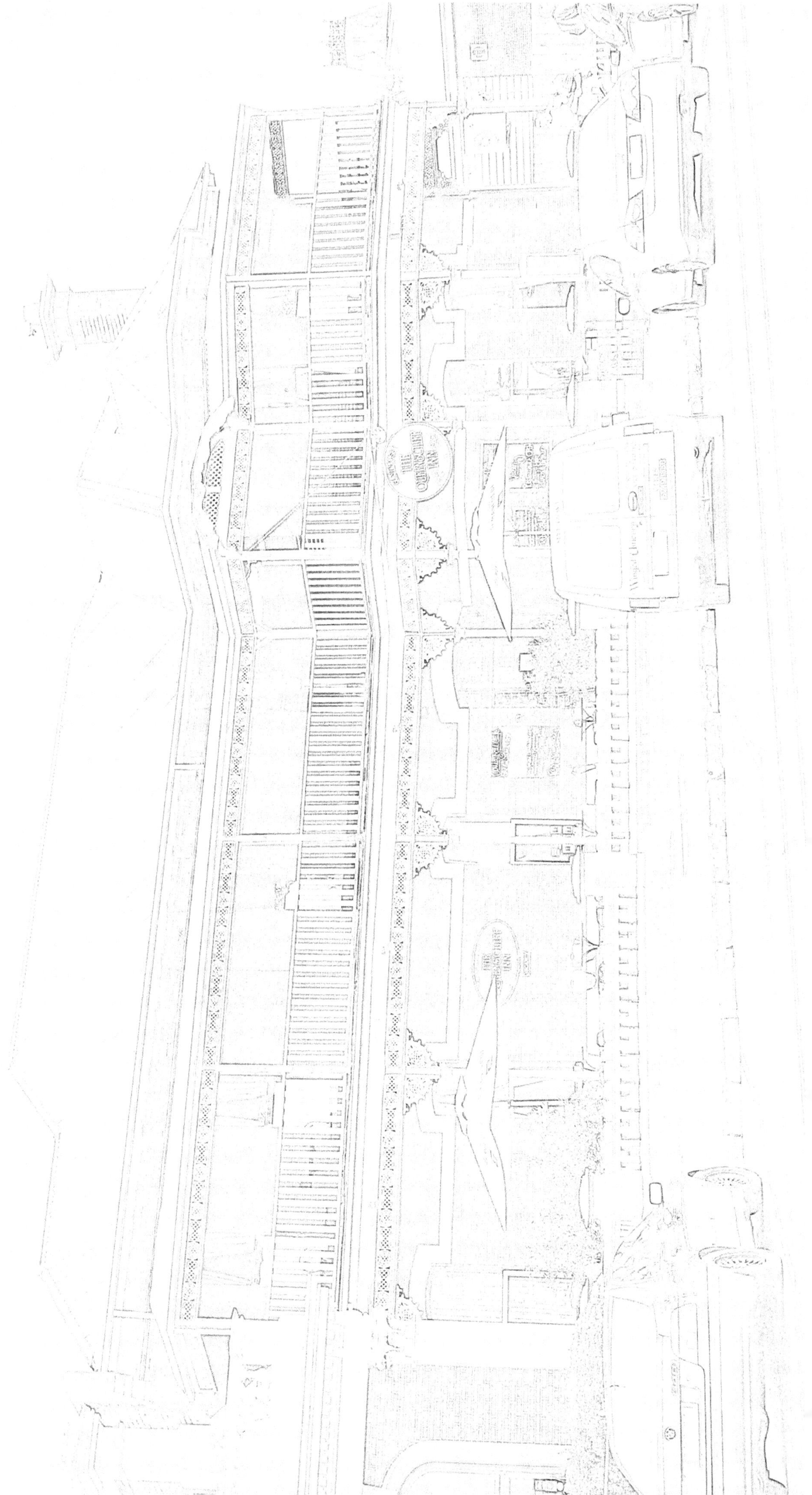

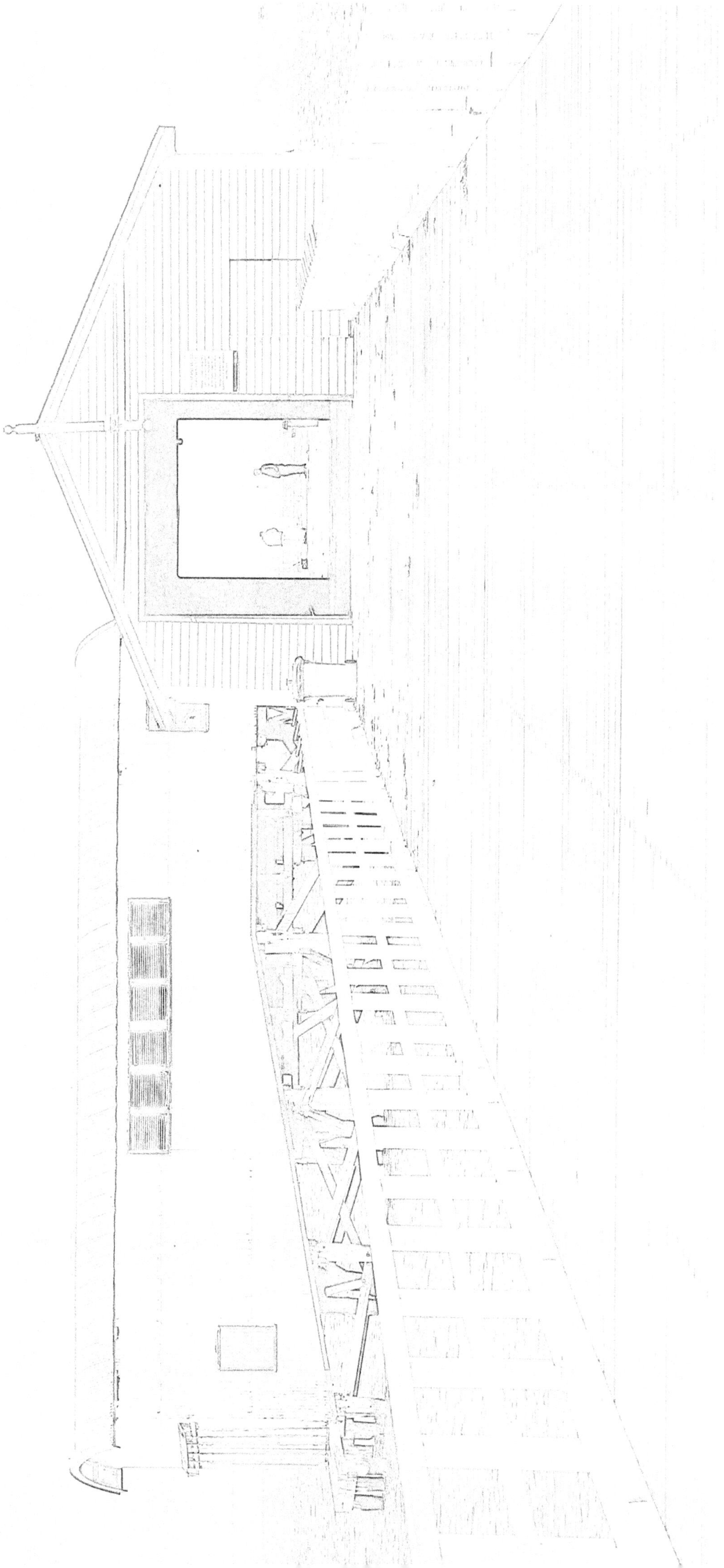

CLEARANCE
4.2m
PT>
SPECTRE

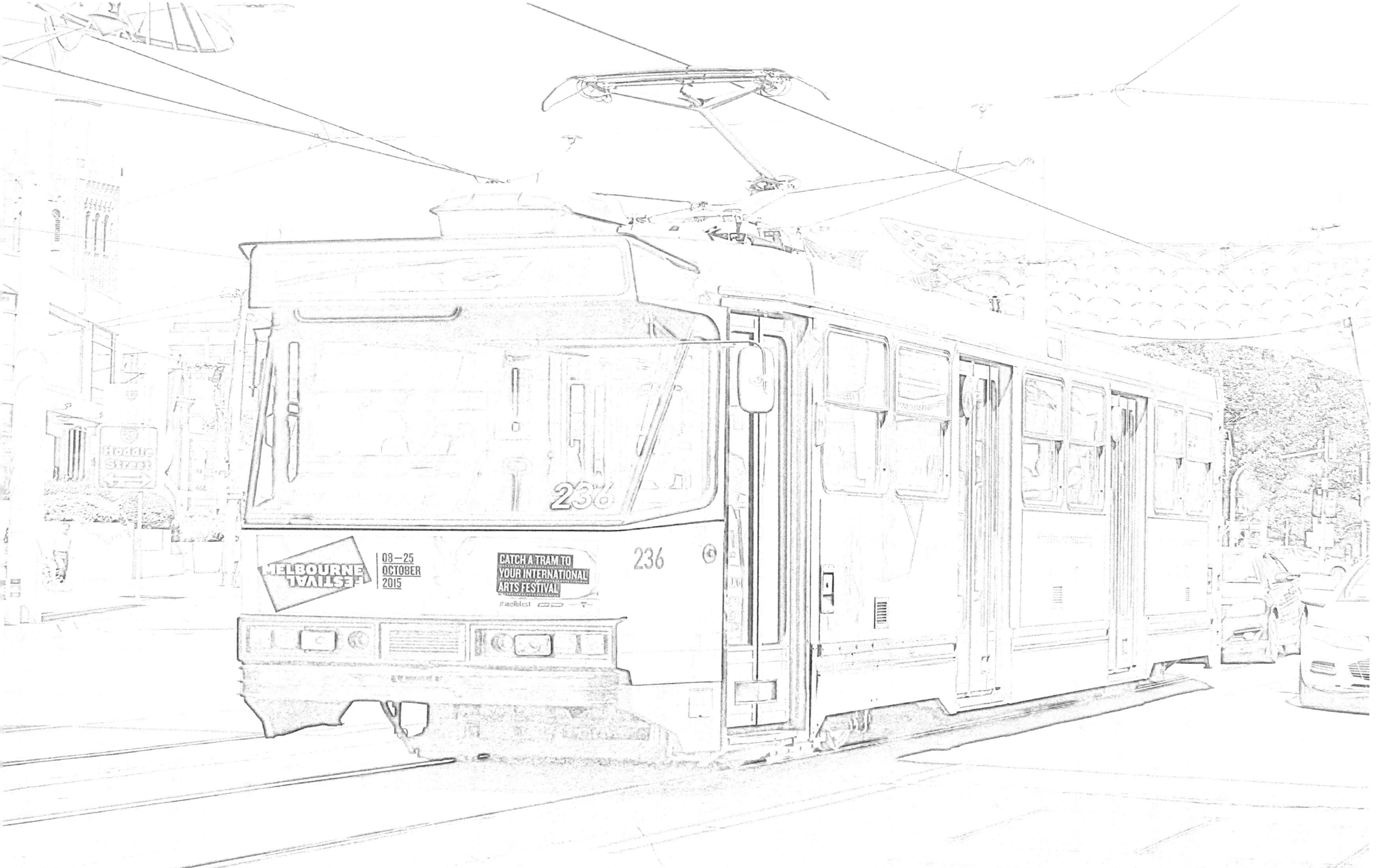
236
MELBOURNE FESTIVAL
08—25 OCTOBER 2015
CATCH A TRAM TO YOUR INTERNATIONAL ARTS FESTIVAL
#melbfest
236
Hoddle Street

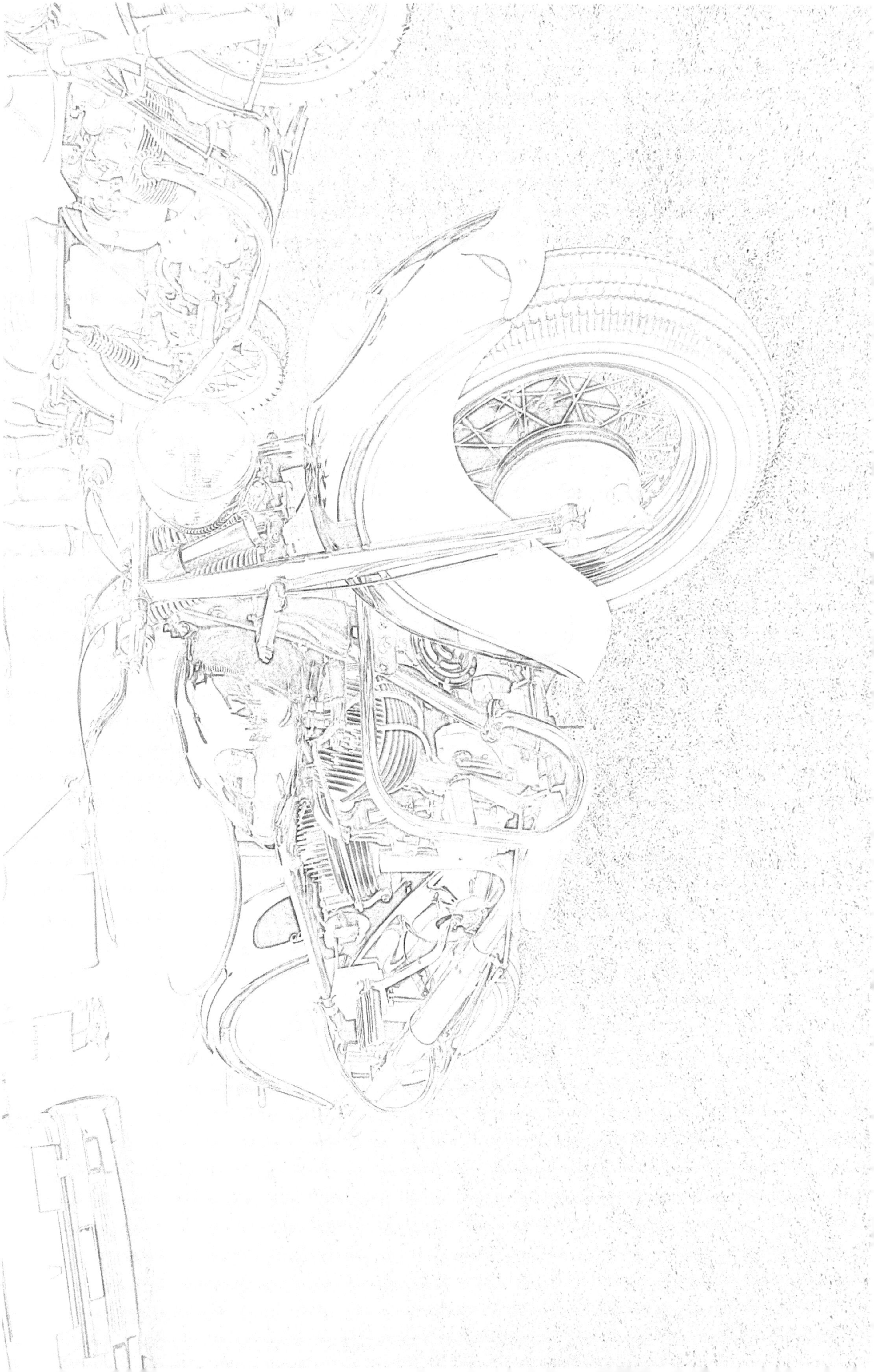

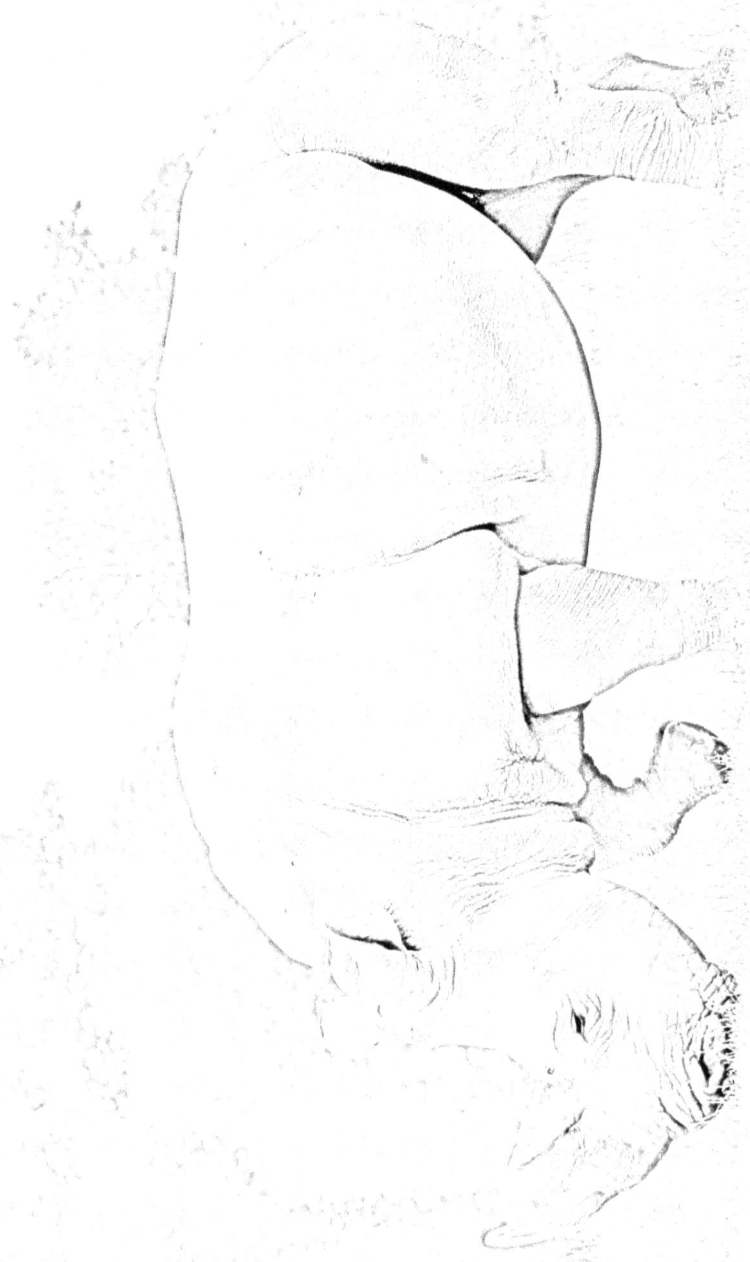

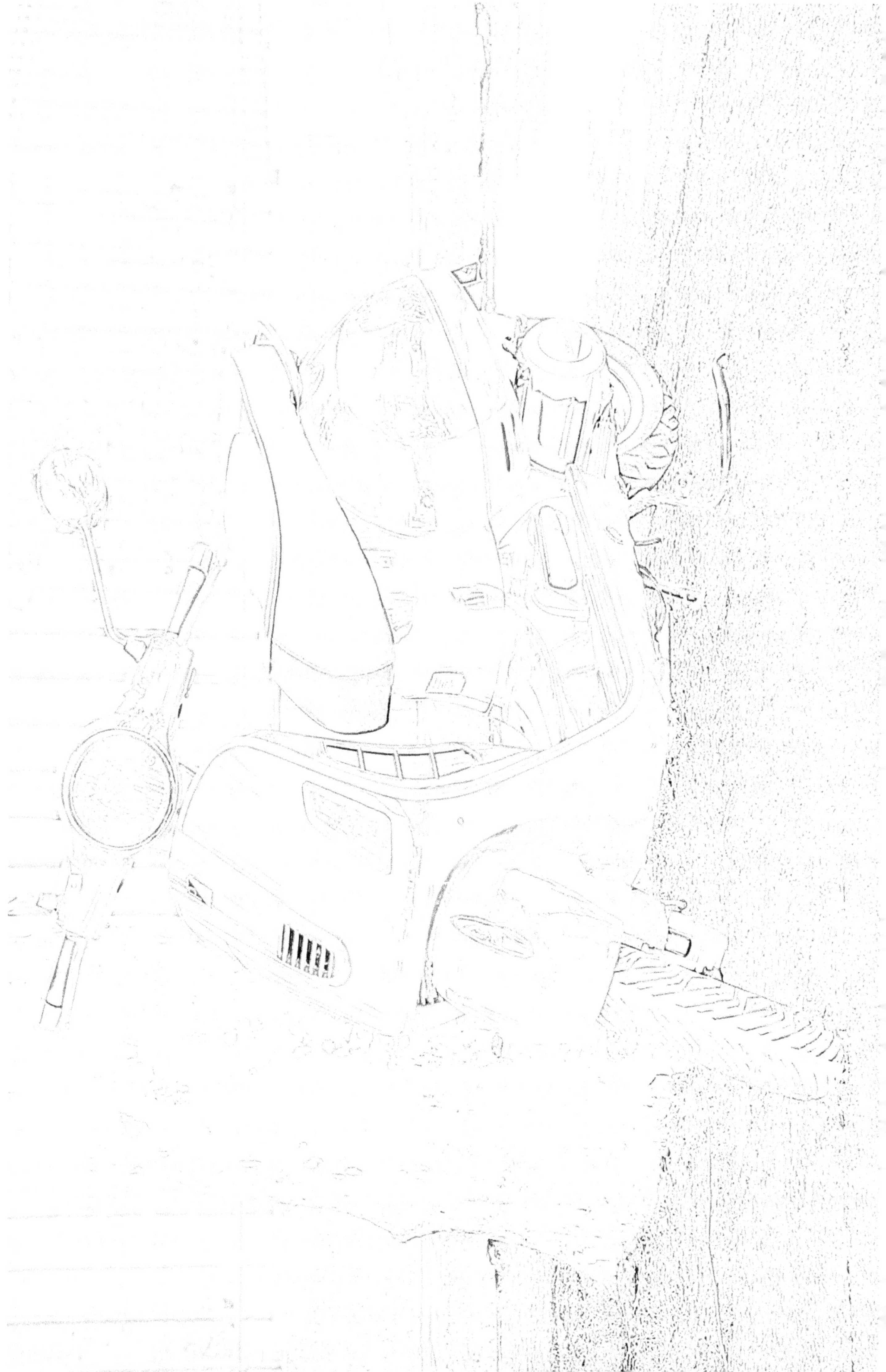

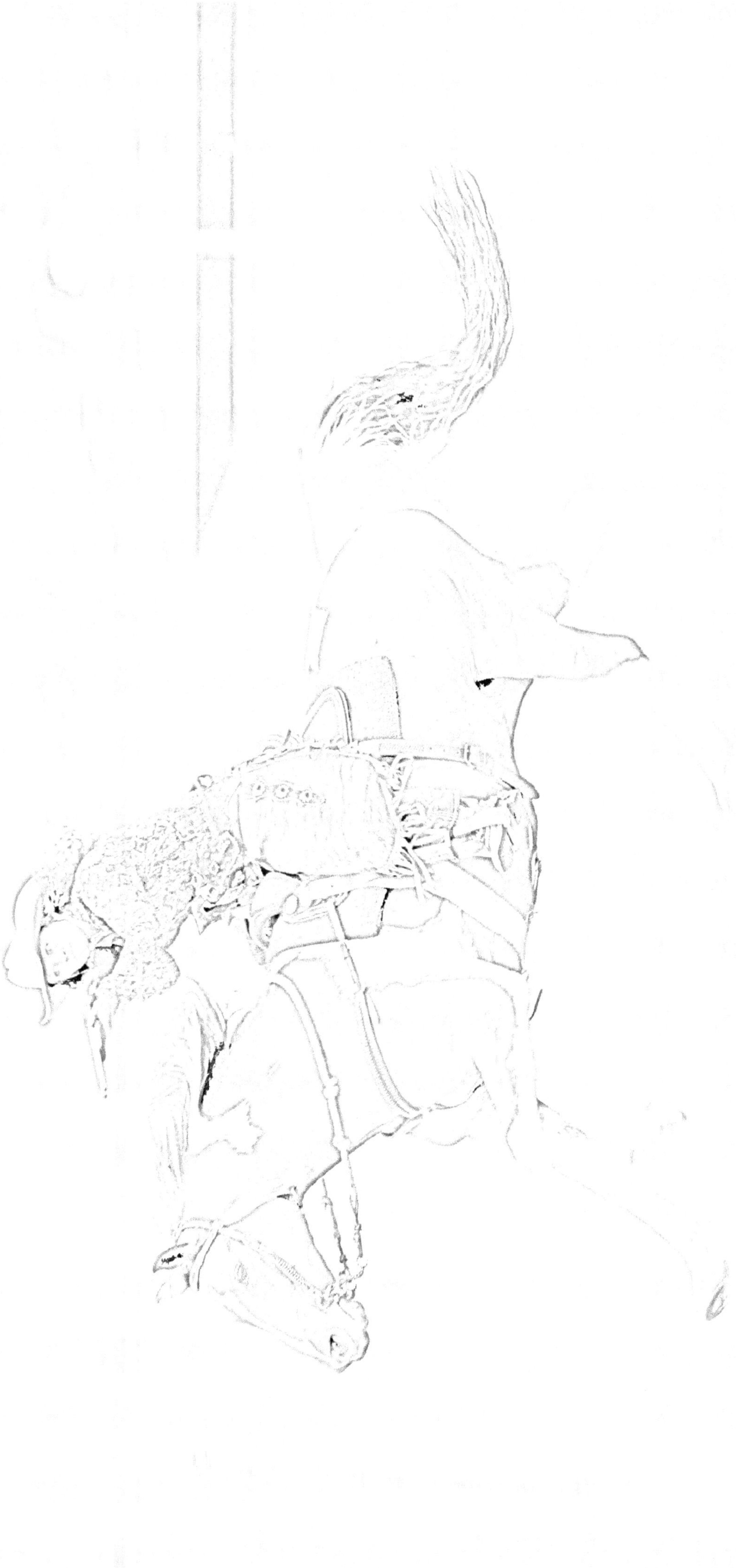

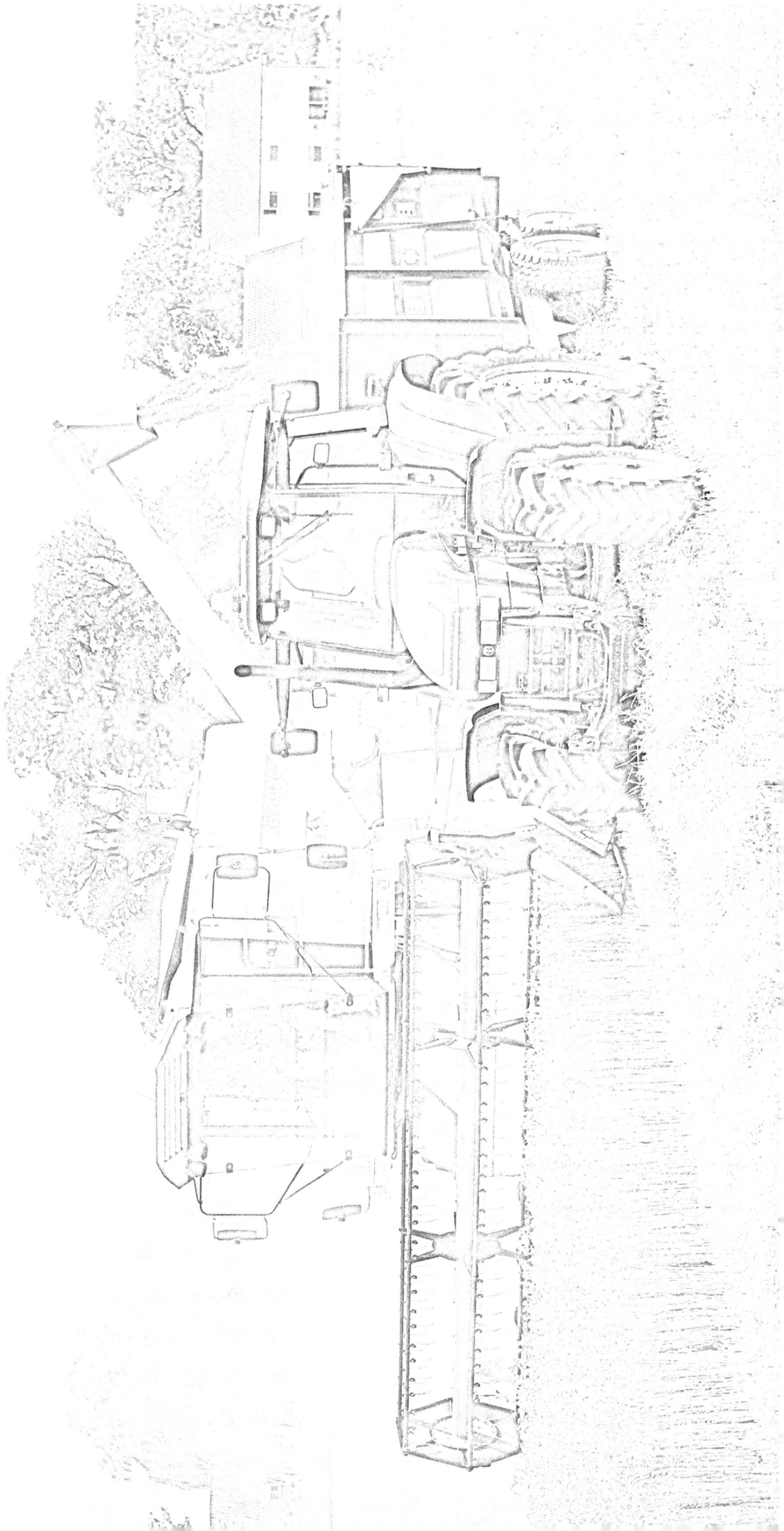

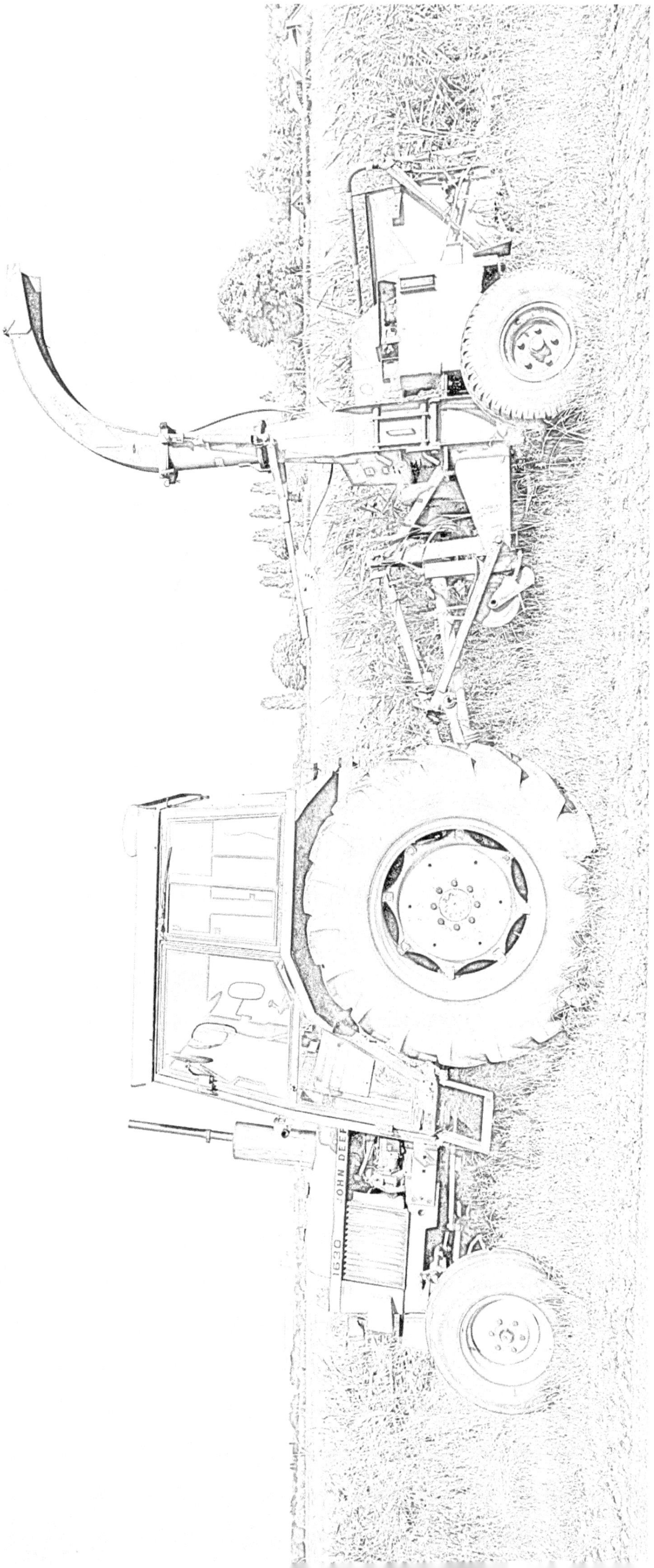

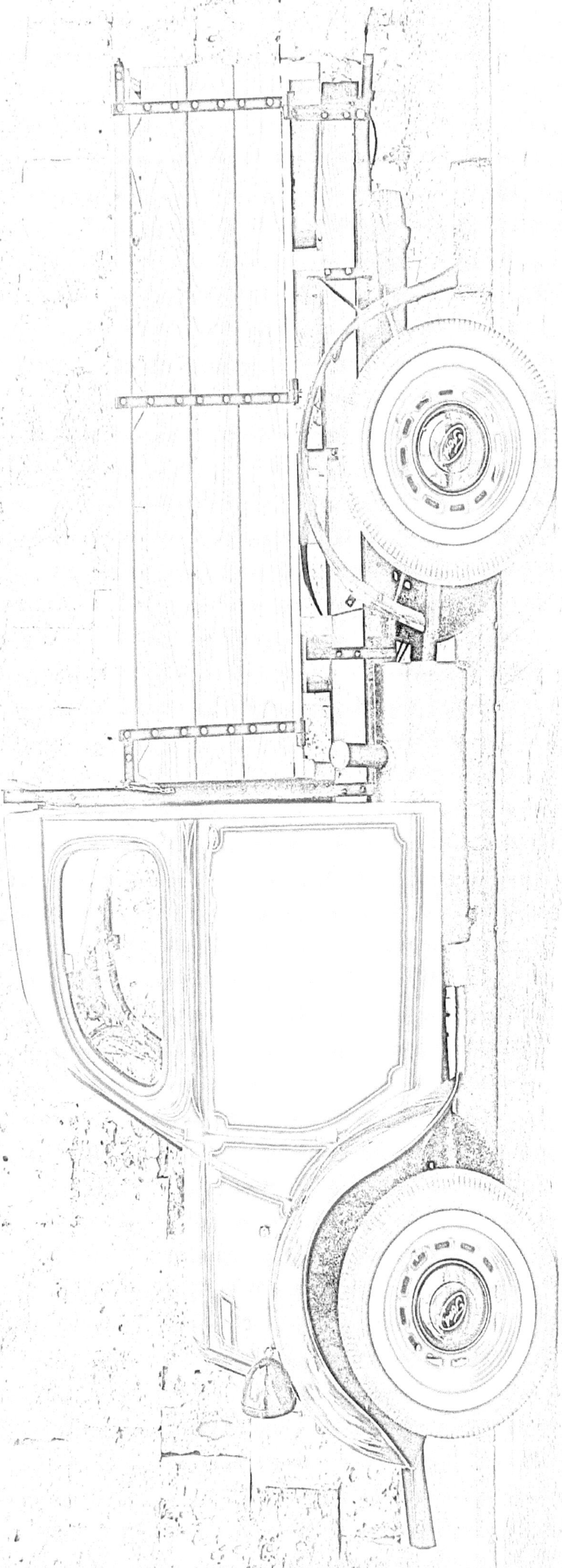

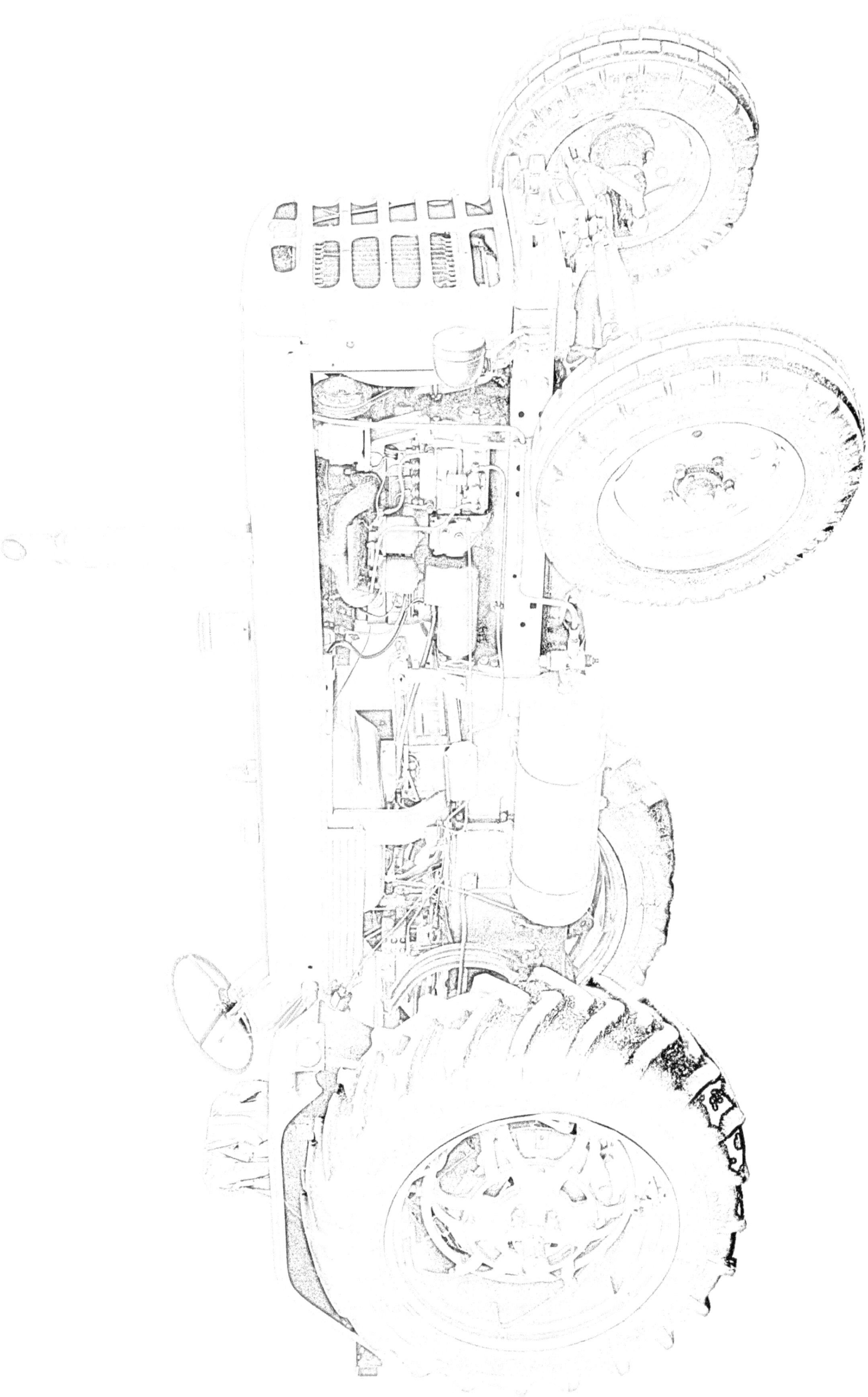

www.ingramcontent.com/pod-product-compliance
Lightning Source LLC
Chambersburg PA
CBHW081056180526
45170CB00005B/1773